*Touching Poem.
One word at a time*

E Hurble Daily

Let's Go For A Short Walk

Mawoshe.

First Ltd ed © Evelyne. Jan 12 18.

Praise for
Let's Go For A Short Walk

Beautifully poignant journey of exploration, connection, and love. Ms. Horelle Dailey skillfully interweaves the transcendent wisdom of heaven with her deep heart story from earth. This book will bring you joy, tears and, most of all, important life lessons.

~Dr. Anita Rosenfield PhD

This is a book requiring the reader's full attention. In doing so, subtleties reveal themselves, and guide the reader into a world filled with peacefulness and meaningful interactions.

~Belle Fergin

Twice I read the book and probably could read it many more times to fully grasp the nature of this remarkable relationship. With open heart and soul Horelle Dailey created a work to give readers a portrait of inquiring minds. Covering from birth, religions, philosophies and a lot more. In this book discussions two old souls began centuries ago continue.

I love at the beginning of the book . . . ambling toward friendship." I could visualize the imprint of tears on many of the pages. *Let's Go for a Short Walk* is a remarkable work of heart.

~Donna Bowing

US Marine

Author of:

The Dues Card

Once in a while a rare book makes its way into the world. It is born out of the fierce storms of life, carrying in its wake tales of love, victory, wisdom and self-mastery.

This is a life-enhancing and life-changing book. It articulates the whisperings of every spirit, hidden beneath the armor we present to the world. Through this journey the narrative brings an extraordinary sense of soul development. Lyrically told, Eveline Horelle Dailey has written a masterpiece.

~Mantoshe Singh Devji

Author of:
The Mad Messiah: Osama Bin Laden and the Seeds of Terror

The Secret Life of Jesus Christ

The Tibetan Gospel of Jesus Christ

The Virgin in Art

Other books by Eveline Horelle Dailey:

The Drum Made From The Skin Of My Sisters

*Lessons from the Lakeside—
A Journey Toward Self Discovery*

The Canvas—A Secret from the Holocaust

Let's Go for a Short Walk

Copyright @ 2017 Eveline Horelle Dailey
All rights reserved. No parts of this book may be reproduced in
any form or by any electronic or mechanical means, including
photocopying,
recording, without the written permission of the publisher, except by a
reviewer, who may quote
brief passages in a review.

Published by EvelineNow
5 West Casa Hermosa Drive
Phoenix, Arizona 85021

Evelinenow@gmail.com

First Edition

ISBN: 978-0-692-90182-3
LCCN: 1- 5278103681

Edited by Jacob Shaver
Cover Design by C. A. Wilke

Contents

Dedication & Front Matter..xi
First Fruits..2
Noticing Attributes...10
 Discoveries of a First Rendez-Vous..............................13
There was Space..18
The Cave...22
Revelation in a Cave...30
Obscurities in Dialogue..34
Let Us Continue About Birth..41
The New Baby Comes Home...45
A Table for Two...52
First Impressions of School..63
A First Communion..68
Saved by Family and Friends..71
There Was a Thief..73
Many Lessons...77
The Sweat Lodge, or The *Inepe*......................................82
A Pin Setter at a Bowling Alley..89
The Erie Canal..97
The Child of an Orphan Train..101
A Mother I Think of Often..111
She Was the Mother of My Children...............................116
Walking and Talking..122

Another Walk Around the Lake	124
What Is the Time?	127
One with Another One	133
Half a Clock	137
Three Quarters of a Clock	142
Living in the Now	147
Move Away from the Past	151
The Essence of the Ancestors	156
Divorce Changes People	161
How AA Changed My Life	164
A Monastic Life	169
A Gun	174
Spencer Abbey	181
Remote Viewing	189
No Ruler and No Gauge	192
Many Interruptions	199
Close to Me	203
Friends and Family Visitation	206
I Read Some Sages	209
The Clock Kept Ticking	212
Finding the Opening	219
The Vision Quest	222
When the Time Comes	229

Dedication

To view this work as a material written posthumously is both correct and incorrect. This embroidery with all its colors is a collaborative work between two people. Privately, he called me Evie, and I called him Donald, Donaldo, Don and sometimes Dailey or Patriarch.

Did I know?
I would find myself when I chose to walk
On the side of a man called
Donald Thomas Dailey?
In a broad sense of the word I perceived him as a Patriarch.
He took my hand
We walked
We talked
We pointed
I found the place of my substance
He said,
"Go through the opening
Find your light"
I went through that opening
I found loose letters of the alphabet

Donald Thomas Dailey
As you suggested that I write it
This is your book and the letters are no longer loose.

A Special Note of Gratitude

Only a young man who knew he was Star Dust could see the sun setting in both his life and that of his grandfather. Bryan Peterson, I thank you for our short conversations and all that you were.

Words of Gratitude

I gave the raw manuscript to friends and also to people I did not know—many pairs of eyes were willing to read my words. Filled with gratitude, I cannot possibly name each. I can assure you that I am eternally grateful for the meaningful inputs they gave to me.

~~~

Though I attended only few critique groups, I want to thank those who gave me encouragement and advise.

~~~

I boast, because I found the words of my reviewers formidable. They are printed here for your consideration.

~~~

I met Jacob Shaver at a junction of light and literacy. I gave him pages to evaluate. I wanted him to take a simple look and give me his impression. The material was a first draft, raw and unpolished. The flesh and the emotions had not gone through any healing processes. The words were out of a soul's torments and pain.

A good friend now, Jacob accepted the challenge of editing this creative memoir. He did so without knowing the distance or the depth of the seas he would cross with me. This fellow traveller questioned my every word until I could clarify Don's and my concepts of living fully as two autonomous beings learning to be better humans. He probed about our philosophies. He inquired about the reasons for our thoughts and beliefs.

Jacob became an agent of more of my tears and laughter.

The book, now in your hand, is a product from my heart made better by the expert edits of Jacob Shaver. What brilliance he has!

~~~

I cannot write words of thanks without including Millicent V. Hay. She was to read for content. Also an editor, she could not escape what

she does so well. She gave me great insights. They gave this book further clarity.

~~~

A man who reads my mind created the cover of this book. He also took care of all necessary details to make this a publishable book. Words of gratitude are a lot less than what I owe Chris Wilke.

~~~

In today's publishing world it took the expertise of Ken Johnson to give this book a home in the electronic world. Thank you Ken!

~~~

In my life I have been privileged to meet a family of choice and heart. Four I cannot forget. Their subtle yet bright lights of wisdom imparted in me the fuel to speak my heart.

I owe many thanks to Sir John M. Soderberg, Ph.D. He sculpted in words the spirit that I am. Rose Winters, the Chief Executive Director of the Foundation for Living Medicine, who gave me food for thoughts.

Take the time to read the back of the book to know their words.

I am a writer because Mrs. Adele Seronde gave me a magic marker and asked me to write a first article about Gardens for Humanity—an organization she founded.

Dr. Gladys T. McGarey, MD. MD (H), known as the Mother of Holistic Medicine, showed me how to capture the gifts from within.

Opening

Before we married we insisted on talking about our many differences. His hair and his beard were white. It was fact enough he was older than me. He talked from an elegant and polished core. I found him to be unburdened by ego. This fascinated me.

My hair was sort of auburn that week; I did not know what color my head of hair was. I purchased hair dyes the way some people purchased bread.

He saw age. I saw cultural differences. I saw eating habits. I became engaged in the melodic intimacy of what he said. I liked his thinking processes. I could listen. I could learn.

While we were not looking, events in our lives changed, features we knew nothing about appeared. Our hair did not change—well mine did—from time to time. Minutes became hours, and days became years. I discovered muscles and bones I did not know I had. He discovered diseases he did not know he would have. They called this time the sunset years. When we saw the sun setting we saw its beauty. Within the individual conditions of our lives we managed to find all that was exquisite in us and around us. That felt good to both of us.

We soon learned to accept the things we could not change, yet for sure, discoveries about ourselves would remain the maxim of our lives. We liked it that way.

We chose to empower ourselves. It took no time at all for me to realize he did that a lot better than I did.

While alive we vowed we would live with happiness of heart, fully and consciously.

To use the word *opening* instead the traditional *foreword* is one of choice. During our journey we learned we could make such choices.

Today I know, *"No matter the length or the width, no one lives without leaving behind the strands of material that made up who they were."*

These words came from a conversation I had with Donald Thomas Dailey. We were talking about the value of a life.

Conversation, events and thoughts created a series of juxtapositions with no particular chronology. Stories came out of their own free flow. I followed suite reflecting on what appeared on a mirror of time and life. Magic presided over the construction of this tome's frame. I may paraphrase when notes are missing or handwriting falters, but this story will be given in sincerity. It will flow in the way of life, with haze and light. An ending with wisdom from near and far will consolidate the book's content.

While I sat in the shadow or sometimes across from a man I often called a patriarch, brilliant and countless conversations took place. Within a circle in time, a staff on-hand—a baton, I called it—stories were revealed. The tales had texture, they were rich; the colorful strands waited for me to weave. Here, articulated with open heart and understanding, a gift has been unpacked. I found a wrapping made from reflections, growth, repetitions, lessons learned, lessons forgotten.

The significance of an existence and its corrections came forth with occasional recurrences. A remarkable and unassuming man expressed his life from acts of giving and kindness. For these qualities, I called him a Patriarch.

Open the door. At the end of the corridor you will find a mirror: take a look.

Let's Go For A Short Walk

A poignant tale of two voices and their conversations on beliefs, adventures, life lessons and philosophies.

Eveline Horelle Dailey

Preface

People, who are storytellers, relate stories and tales fastened to their lives with threads of joy and pain. They tell of their families and friends, mentors and adversaries, all intertwined with all that is mundane, sublime or wounded. They tell stories, and we both did just that.

My part in this chronicle was to extricate the words of a man who lived his life to better himself so he could serve others with grace and anonymity. He often said his aim was to be *better, better than before*. It was years later that I understood what it was to be *better, better than before*. It was simply a matter of mind control.

With many stories to remember, I developed the habit of taking notes during conversations. His life was a dénouement that brought me awe, laughter and tears. The waterworks rolling down my cheeks often found their way between the lines. I was in the presence of a man, not a stranger to deep emotions. He used those to guide his deeds. I dare say he was an awakened being.

It took only moments after our first encounter to notice, he was a man of intellect—that was pleasing. He was not religious—that felt good. A while later, I discovered a self-mastery that in the façade he concealed. He was a spiritual man, and early in our relationship I could not isolate this characteristic to any given philosophies. There was something deep inside that seemed to give him an opening he appeared to count on. I was puzzled by this orderly personality.

Around him I felt comfortable and unburdened!

My life of many endeavors in the hotel design industry placed me nationally in and out of boardrooms, and often a suitcase was my home. Together with other designers I made attempts at divining within budget and style what was most suited inside various hotels. Glamorous to the untrained eye, this was a hard life. Travels, lunches, dinners and meaningless conventions were parts of my professional life. This existence was, however, filled with a great deal of time and was not

always fun. My life also came with relentless hours of grueling effort to satisfy the needs of my clients and of course, my monetary gains.

What I did on a professional basis took hours of days and nights, but did not identify who I was. My private life however, was a guided one, and continues to be so. A property by a creek became my home in the high desert. Adventuresome always, my next exploration took me to an organization planting gardens in schools, hospitals and pocket parks. I soon became the Vice President of Gardens for Humanity. In a life with natural flow, and a desire for beauty around me, art and artists magically squeezed themselves into fulfillment of my time and life. I was surrounded by what gave me pleasure. An art gallery became an extension of all that I did.

It was the natural setting of my home that also made my way of living attractive. I could dance in joy and harmony. I had three acres I did not need, and fruit trees producing more than I could ever consume. Born of these things came a center to expand my world. Neighbors, including visitations by members of a small clan of the Apache Nation, visited and helped themselves to the bounties of the land. To better adorn this magical place, a labyrinth a hundred and forty-four feet across found its center on the property. A master douser was responsible for its placement on the land. It was not a replica of the one found at Grace Cathedral in San Francisco, nor was it like the one in Chartres Cathedral in France. It was an ancient design with seven-coil, representing the seven days of the week, or the planets and much more. This design can still be found in most countries, from Crete to Egypt, Nepal to Tibet, France, and of course here in the USA. To me, this labyrinth symbolized the mysteries of life itself. The path was entered from one *opening* and the exit was the same. Meandering the circles and finding my own center became a moving meditation. This action was akin to many Buddhist and also Zen monks walking the path one step next to the other. This simple exercise demanded complete attention to self. People from all states and many countries were aware of its placement on the global map of labyrinths. Visiting strangers, walking, chanting and/or meditating along its *unicursal* pattern, a clever word used to describe the circular shape of this labyrinth became a normal occurrence on the property. Its

only entry and exit may have symbolized something different to those walking its path.

My home, much like the rest of the property, was fairly large for one individual. I believe in accordance, and because of universal laws of abundance, three artists in residence became part of this setting. The place by the creek was filled with magic.

The water from the creek I set my feet in came from a tributary of the Well of Montezuma.

The gods of the indigenous Sin Agua ensured that the temperature of the flowing water would remain at around seventy-eight degrees all year. The same gods, however, neglected the outside temperatures during the winter months. Often I promised myself; one day I would have a talk with them about the simple matter of temperature. Alas, I never learned their language.

My character and the tempo of my life presented me with challenges to crack open. I learned from each opening the joy of being. I identified who I was becoming on a daily basis.

It was during this period of time in my life, on a long walk, at the edge of a different path, that I began to observe not only the object of a first encounter, but myself within each step taken. Listening to well spoken words during a walk, I found myself pleased. I had been given the tools to know that this man did not arrive to the place of grace I was noticing without accepting and conquering difficulties such as chaos and trauma in his life. Later on I was to find out what secrets he held.

Without many words or efforts, Donald Dailey gave me glimpses of how he lived his own truth. Soon enough, I knew if this friendship flourished, I would have to unravel some mysteries.

The many turns of a life took us for a dance; an agreeable tempo dictated the steps we took. The sound of many instruments paused. Lessons in acceptance had to be learned for we were different in many ways. It came a time when a difficult period began; it was mixed with bliss and final challenges. Not prepared just yet, he asked me to assist him with a phase of his journey—our journey. The end of his life was near, and the time to let words and emotions flow freely was upon us. To take on this task, and its challenges thereof, became the greatest honor I ever received.

By some means not yet clear to me, I knew I had to package eighty-six years of this private man's life. Realizing that all structures needed origination and concept, I tunneled through what I knew to be a foundation. Coming upon an opening, I found when it was time to examine all that was.

Based on stories he had told me about his early life, I began to write. It took no time at all, and the spell of writing had to take a holiday. I read to him my account of his birth. He was lying on his hospital bed in our home.

The path we walked thus far had turned—we followed the arrow on the road, and our lives changed. He smiled, his hazel eyes looking at me with a touch of satisfaction. I could detect his particular smile behind the beard. He pondered a while and said:

"You have a wonderful way with imagination. You see in me as a lot more than what is here. I am just a man, Evie, a dying man at that. You, my dear, are kind. You imagine matters of birth to escape the matter of death. A good distraction, yours or mine—there is a question here for both of us."

"No, Donald, based on what I heard from you and your sisters, I allowed the words to do what words do."

Our lives were filled with laughter. He said he was amused by my spontaneity and my passion for life. My dancing around the house with earphones on gave him the impression that I transformed myself to a robot or a mime. He was not a man enamored with wild or passionate music. He said I gave him a show each time I had my earphones on. I told him it was all for his therapy, and sometimes mine.

There was balance in our lives, and sometimes we cried during our sessions. I had been taking more notes, and the gusto of life made

way for the flow of tears. For me, there was something magical about being in the presence of an awakened being. The very idea of having that magic gone was difficult to accept. He showed me how to dare to live fully, even while understanding the impermanence of all things.

There were pauses in our conversations, and each time I wondered if this was his way of giving me occasion for digestion.

"The son of Mini, imagine that. My mother would have liked you Evie. She probably wouldn't have understood you, but I know she would have liked you. She was a small woman, thus came the name Mini. She had a heart filled with compassion. I see that in you, though you are intrepid and spontaneous, reckless and critical and arrogant too. I know she would have adored you, yet she was none of those things. I am amused when you say with conviction that who you are is all about your birthrights. You are a sure-footed woman, a matter of upbringing I suspect—I like you Evie, more than you will ever know. I also love you, because you have become the love of my long life."

This man, whom I often referred to as magnanimous, did not know how powerful he was. As an author, I found noteworthy content in his stories and his life. The collage brought me a tapestry, a tree of life.

As we went along with the writing project, he decided to remove many stories and add a few more. This desire was respected here.

We were two distinct people with separate voices, and yet there were threads to bind the intricacies of our spirits. We each learned to use them well.

Let's Go For
A Short Walk

Eveline Horelle Dailey

First Fruits

There is not always time to ponder about lives, yet in Don's and mine, there are some flashes I remember vividly. Our exchanges were followed by reflections of times past. The necessity to visit the future was not essential; it was not a place where we travelled often. Our lives would magically stretch themselves to rearrange the environment where my mind would meet his.

The universe must have had plans outside the norm when we met. We were both students of our own, yet different, spiritual pursuits. We made sure that the unintentional demands of our lives did not reduce the importance of our development.

It was a year after an accidental meeting orchestrated by friends that our relationship took a turn that would change both our lives. A telephone call, a probing about my likes and dislikes, became the guiding hints that got me on a walk with a man whom in fact, I did not know. Curiously enough, there was a trail near my home I was not familiar with, yet he knew it well. I had been sufficiently aware of my own guidance to know not to ignore this moment. My schedule that day was tight, yet I felt that time would stretch itself to allocate a pleasurable moment to walk on a trail.

Juniper and Creosote flanked the route and created the particular aroma of Arizona's high desert. A search for the source of Montezuma

Well was the focus of this walk. While the winds of a March afternoon under the blue sky perfumed the air, an invisible orchestra of wind instruments played enchanting melodies to delight my senses. I could hear the music of the wild. The terrain we walked allowed for particular instances of mysterious revelations. Conversations including pleasantries and ideas about life in general, followed our footsteps.

Creatures of the desert entertained us; sometimes a small bug triggered conversation about survival. This land held and gave ways to dialogues about differences such as culture and age. We talked about how we maneuvered our lives and found out that we were people focused on personal growth with a penchant for fun. My kind of fun was not necessarily his. He was a retired man who had a great deal of enjoyment when he worked. I worked non-stop at more than one endeavor, and also had fun every minute. We both understood the joy and the risks of being self-employed.

More than once that afternoon conversation took us outside our comfort zone. Each time we acknowledged the obvious. We were very different by reasons of cultures. We continued to probe deeper into our psyches. Perhaps at the time we seemed to have been looking for a possible ray of friendship. This encounter was one not romantically inclined.

During the analytical moments of our first encounters character and temperament were exposed to the light. Without effort pacing farther along the trail, we were soon sharing the secrets of our souls and differences thereof.

There was a sort of ease of dialogue approaching which I found puzzling. The feeling did not suggest that we stop talking. Something I could not identify, because he was not like any man I had ever met, left me rather perplexed. Was it his exquisite manners? Was I looking for cultural differences I knew had to be hidden somewhere? We were, after all, from different worlds. It was a glorious day, so we continued the walk, only to realize the destination was impossible to find. The source of the well was hidden from our view.

Differences that came with languages and backgrounds demanded reflection and sometimes explanations. The territories we speculated about were unfamiliar, yet later encounters formulated the makings of an engagement with future time.

We each managed our lives well, we knew how to build fortresses and protect what we recognized as the wholeness of our individual autonomy. We found our individual comfort zone important to our way of living.

Without conscious effort our variety of exchanges grew more frequent. We had no particular agenda; we simply enjoyed each other's conversations and company.

We walked on as if we had a key to a doorway to be opened or closed as we pleased. There was something freeing behind that door. We were finding elements of conversation entering the metaphysical or cosmic attributes. We had not approached such subjects. We did not know each other well enough, I suppose. Many questions not yet posed were gaining momentum. At the time, neither of us knew that wild and profound answers would follow.

I believed we employed our own correctness to express our self-assurance.

Years later, he told me how charmed he had been by the fact that I took life's many challenges and its pleasures for granted. He was amused because I believed that all good things were part of my birthright, and when life presented me with challenges, I considered the fact that I was going through a rite of passage.

No one ever told me differently. How else could I possibly view my life?

Walking side-by-side on this accommodating trail, we talked nonstop. At times I mentally questioned if we had not been suffering from a lack of intelligent and engaging conversations.

He told me he was raised a Roman Catholic and at a very young age his mother dedicated him to the church. He explained that especially

in poor Irish Catholic families this was a common occurrence. They did that in order to serve the church and provide education for their sons. I was astonished. In my life, I had not met people so devoted to a church. He would have ended up in a seminary to become a priest if they had not moved away from New York State. This was difficult to fathom. I was facing a person with cultural differences distinctly unfamiliar to me.

A few more steps, and an area of new vegetation appeared not far from us. The junipers gave way to taller evergreens. He said a few words I did not hear. I was mentally engaged in matters of religions. I was attempting to understand the demands and the gifts such institutions made on people. I then heard him say something about being puzzled by my Buddhist tendencies and having no particular religion. We both must have been thinking about similar subjects. I was as baffled by his story about the priesthood as he was about my Buddhist philosophies. It was my turn to explain my views about many things.

"I came from a Catholic society, yet elements of Islam and Judaism were also part of the bastion from which I grew. In my world, people knew about the value of money in churches and temples to acquire desired results. The influences of Spain's Catholic or Islamic tenor were alive with my mother's people. After all, Islam occupied Spain for seven hundreds years, therefore, it was a given that many things in the Spanish world grew out of Islam. Look at South America's architecture, or right here in Arizona, look at the many arches found in homes. Look at the rounded doors. Look at the tiles we use on our roofs. Few people know about such facts. This amuses me, but I know in my family the use of a purse with money inside dictated many outcomes. I do not believe any of that has changed. I find following Buddhist principles are easier on my persona.

He looked shocked or puzzled—I could tell. I had to bring clarity to my point and to do so, I explained about my first marriage. This young bride wanted to be married at St. Patrick's Cathedral because in New York it was the most splendid place I could think of. My desire was not an act of devotion, but one of ego. I do not know what sum of money was paid, but I did marry my first husband at the Cathedral. To my explanation, I added that as far as I knew, it was the way money changed outcomes. I was not a member of that church. I could tell he did not expect such an explanation, but accepted it.

We continued our walk, this time discussing my living in the *now*. He was interested in how I learned to carry on life in a detached way. To him, not attempting to control outcomes would make me a victim, but he said he realized I was not. He could tell I worked for and focused on the things I wanted. I was glad he could tell I was not one to wait for miracles. My concept of living in my *now* would suffer much interference. He told me upon leaving the Catholic Church he began to study other religions. He read some Eastern philosophers and found wisdom in the words of Lao Tzu, but found the passive processes of their lives foreign to anything he knew or found comfort in. His youth came with rules, the rigidity of Rome, and also Ireland and poverty. It was evident our upbringing molded us with distinct and different markers.

I quickly discovered he planned his life with marvelous direction, caution, and wisdom. I also noticed some spontaneity. The differences between us were great, yet we were finding harmony in our conversations. I explained further about the personal concepts of Buddhism we had talked about. To me life was like seeing everything as a river of pure water, and that water carried with it virtues that were not visible to the naked eye, but they could be felt. I explained I did not mean this in a wrong or right way of doings, but rather as a state of being that worked for me. He had a wonderful way of looking at me when he was puzzled by what I said. He had a crooked smile only a few could see. To that I offered the best explanation I could. With my hands in front of me, I told him to imagine them cupped and filled with water. I would not be able to control the water and make it stay put. The water would slip right through my fingers. Fluid like life itself, the water had to do what it does best, and go where it needed to go. For me that was Buddhism. I needed to only do my best and control nothing.

We kept on walking. I wondered why he needed me as a companion. He was an avid hiker, and it was evident, I was not. With nonchalance he told me the first time we met he found my foreignness fascinating.

In business he had met a few foreign women, but never one in business for herself. He found me forceful and he wanted to find out what made me tick. My understanding of patriotic endeavors and the fact that I had chosen to become an American enthralled him. I did not respond to his observations. I was not sure I understood the fascination. As for forceful, I did not see myself as such; confident perhaps.

My approach to life was different from his. I listened to the music of far-away violins, mixed with the classic guitars of my mother's people. In my life, it was the beat of the tambourine that kept order to my verve. He had little interest in music, something I found difficult to understand. I came to consider this to be the result of an early life in poverty. The fundamental ways of my daily life that I took for granted in my upbringing had not been part of his. Our lives and their circumstances were not the same.

We kept on talking. We kept on taking short walks.

I realized as he spoke of his youth there were no musical instruments around him. No philharmonic concerts to attend. No operas that I dreaded but had to go to. In his life there were no painting or dance classes. These things all in the name of culture were routine in my life, but absent in his. He wanted to learn to play the piano but was told by the school's music teacher, a nun: "poor people do not play the piano". I could see the sadness in his entire being when he told me this story.

I could not believe such a statement came from a nun. I was under the impression that they were people with compassion; obviously this one came without heart or conscience.

We were walking on a narrow path when he told me the piano story. He said it had been over seventy years since the event. I became aware—this unkind and adverse pronouncement left belittling damages behind.

Faced with this reality, I have since given a great deal of thought to the many words I have spoken to others. There has been time when the words spoken were without an ounce of concern. I am glad that this young boy, despite the very poverty that prevented him from playing the piano, made the necessary efforts to surmount the adverse conditions of his early life. Standards set by the society he was born into did not prevent him from becoming a successful adult. Poverty did not affect his life or the life of his children.

We had been married about ten or so years when he purchased a synthesizer. He wanted to learn to play the piano. He took lessons. He understood the placement of the keys, but alas, after so many years without music, he found, it was not only his voice that could not carry a tune, he was tone deaf. He sold the synthesizer and once in a while sang me a few bars of Old Men River. He did that surprisingly well.

All along there was more than a touch of comfort and fun during our walk: we were being real. This was not something I had experienced with anyone. This man was not making attempts at impressing me.

We walked on.

We had a good laugh when he asked me what I did when the *now* I spoke of was over. Since we were walking when he asked, my answer came out in one breath.

"Well, Donald, there is always another now, see? I take a step that is a now. I take another step. It is another now, and I do not know where my foot will land. To me that is the way of my life. Taking each step, hoping I will not fall, and if I do, knowing how to get up again. For me, astonishing things happen when I arrange my life that way. When I am thirsty I drink, one gulp for each cardinal direction. I attribute this to my ceremonial indigenous teachings and also the teachings from the East. One day, I must tell you of my times at the sweat lodges. By the way, the structure is called an *Inepe*.

"One day, I will tell you about my sweating experiences and also my vision quest. This came during a period of intense inner growth in my life. I spent two years going to the lodge at night, during the full moon. Indigenous people call the moon *Grand Mother*. You must understand, in my family we do not sweat! So many things, we do not do in my family.

"Now back to numbers. When I am very thirsty, I count to seven for the days of the week and the water knows what to do. Cosmic numbers mean something to me, but I am not a numerologist. I only try to understand the movement of the cosmos. I believe in the energetic power of numbers to control everything. You have to admit it works better than when people attempt to control all things."

It was during one of our hikes that I brought up my labyrinth. I noticed he had intensely looked at this series of circles while waiting for me.

"I bet you saw my labyrinth when you came to pick me up. One day, if we meet again, I will walk the circles with you."

"So you understand about circles, too? Eveline, you are really amazing. I am glad you agreed to go for a walk with me. I am enjoying this. Your conception of life is different from what I have been exposed to. Am I understanding while you go about the business of your life, in the silence of your mind you are counting all the time? I feel you are passionate about all that you do. It appears that you really dance to that tambourine of yours. You will have to teach me about how you live, especially that *now* thing and the *Inepe* also."

"Yes, I count all the time. For one thing, it keeps my mind on what my hands are doing. If our friendship grows, I will learn a great deal from the way *you* control *your* life. I will also show you how I live mine."

Without hesitation he said, "*I know our friendship will grow.*"

Noticing Attributes

We took time to digest conversations. The subjects jumped like the crickets we encountered. We were at ease with each other, yet comfortable alone. I trust we both felt good about who we were. Our walk told me he was a man of measure and mental order. He exercised a sense of discipline that appeared to have been learned. There was also something humble that emerged as part of his core. I felt no rigidity of character. We talked about my newly discovered impression of him; he retorted that he was stubborn. Irish people are said to be that way, he told me. He also said they used this as some sort of an excuse for bad behavior.

"I am not sure my roots have anything to do with stubbornness. I don't like changes."

"Donald, I believe when there is change, one loses control unless, of course, they initiated the change. It's control some of us do not like to lose."

The way he looked at me, I knew I had touched a cord. I recognized it because I also did not like it when people trespassed or touched the cords that made me tick. He must have been very attached to his ideas of control.

Let's Go For A Short Walk

We continued to walk on the trail that was not too difficult, despite the fact that I was not wearing the proper shoes. He seemed to have known every pebble and rock intimately. He pointed to some boulders with odd shapes and with tenderness showed me new saplings. I found him to be a sensitive man with a penetrating core that he probably did not allow too many people to see. He was at ease speaking about his real estate business, and about his exploits before retirement. There was reservation in more personal areas. This was appropriate since he did not know me well enough for much else. We were just *ambling toward friendship*.

For sure this man mystified me. He was a gentleman. He sensed he was not to hold my elbow, arm or hand; I would have reacted unfavorably. He was observant enough to know my sense of freedom was reactive. Yet the occasional hug with laughter was acceptable. Anything else would have been intrusive.

My life experiences placed me on the feminist side of things. I was also feminine and was comfortable with my femininity. I was, however, rather capable of taking my own steps no matter where they led me. I did not need to know him well to determine he was a man who observed all that was around him. He was as at ease with himself and his stories as I was with mine. A man of rare charm, I felt.

There was something pleasing about discovering his sense of self. My past experiences had placed me with people with a need bent on pleasing others to get what they wanted. I would say he was a person who did not answer to others. This was an interesting characteristic we both held, and yet, we were different.

We walked on. There are so many discoveries to be made when two people go walking, destination unknown.

As we traversed from one conversation to the next, I also noticed how well groomed he was. Spotless white sneakers, not new ones but clean ones, not a spec on the white. That told me a great deal about him. His pale blue pair of jeans of perfect fit and his long sleeved shirt of a blue one shade lighter than the pants he wore were all pressed. It takes a special man to either have his clothes pressed or to press them himself. The attire he wore framed his 6' 2" well. The blue of his shirt gave life to his perfectly cut head of gray. His well manicured beard was one suggestion of gray darker than his full head of particularly shinny hair. I noticed the hazel color of his eyes had a great deal of depth. There was clarity about them, not in the color, but in something I could not name.

I was experiencing an odd but well received feeling. I was enjoying being with this man. For a moment I became aware of being attracted to him. I smiled; maybe it was because he was so well groomed.

In contrast to him, there I was with my flowing midi-skirt of colorful cotton paisley printed in India. A multitude of sequins reflected the sun. My peasant blouse and my gold sandals gave me the air of a gypsy, a state of mind and heart I seemed to have had embraced long ago. There was no mistake. We were different, "vive la différence" I thought. Accepting things dissimilar was the way of life I was comfortable with. Being a man who paid attention to the word "future" I therefore understood why he did not understand my "now".

We kept on walking, observing and talking more.

The high desert trail changed here and there, much like life, I remarked. A few pine trees showed themselves; they were struggling to survive the terrain. Their shade of green was not verdant enough. The wind and the birds continued a variety of melodies.

This was a good walk. Alas like all things, the walk had to end, for my time to open the art gallery for my spring equinox exhibition was near.

Discoveries of a First Rendez-Vous

"You know Evie, as always, I talk too much. I jump from one subject to the other and I may never be able to keep time of events straight. Come to think of it, you do the same. Who knows? One day we will both work on that. In the meantime, you told me about writing something about my birth. Where is it? You told me about it more than once. I am curious to know what you wrote. I would like to see it. Do you really have it written somewhere? If so, I'd like you to read it to me."

"Don, of course I have it. Give me a moment. I will find it and read it for you. You are always talking about talking too much. Now you will have to deal with my French accent. You know, I do not hear it when I speak, but when I read, words do not sound English. So brace yourself."

"While you are looking for it, find the sweat lodge story too. What did you call it again?"

"It is called an *Inepe*, and you go inside of it. The center of it gets filled with red, and blue hot, large rocks. I went in to sweat."

Many such talks came of the state of abstractions in our conversations and our lives. I will add, also, with no regards for the last discussion we had. It was their momentum that gave us a sense of renewal. It was early on in our relation and our marriage that long tête-à-têtes became part of our daily routine: *Something we felt would be beneficial to most couples.*

Since I was to write with him and for him, the time had come to read my first take. I explained that I viewed our place in the world with its beginning as sperm and womb. I began my reading to him with my idea of preconception.

By his look, I could tell he was puzzled. But again, my husband was often mystified by my views of the world.

Attentively, he listened to my jabber. He was a talker, but also one who knew how to listen. He granted me his attention with considerable interest. The effects of Parkinson's disease were under control. The tremors around his lips with the aid of some medicines were slight. His fingers, however, could no longer be used to type or to write well. We often wondered how easy it was to stop when I held his hands. We attributed all this to the fact that his was a slight case that had not yet totally affected his motor skills or his brain. For that we were both very grateful. I was in constant amazement to witness how well he accepted the various diseases he had.

While his body was failing him he had no problems telling me stories, and many were jewels. I could weigh their brilliance in my hands and between my fingers. Like water from the tap, I could feel the flow but I could not manage to hold onto the ocean. After all, anyone over eighty-five years of age had seen and experienced a great deal. The sharpness of his dazzling mind secured a position for us to continue our limited engagement.

He chose not to worry about the state of his health. He had enough diseases and gave them numbers not as a means of identification, but just for fun or momentary denial. When least expected, a heart with many ailments made itself more visible. Leaky valves, atrial fibrillation, an aorta with a leak, and chordae that were no longer hanging onto the right parts of the heart were only part of the problems with this aging muscle. He already had given one kidney to cancer and the other was getting tired of having to clean residues from medicines. His lungs decided to join and form a trio. I became good at the dance and the music of a caretaker. Both lungs pretended to be like those of a smoker. The specialist that gave names to diseases gave us a new catch phrase: *COPD*. Uninformed and ignorant, the good nurse translated for us, Chronic Obstructive Pulmonary Disease. What was there to obstruct? No one ever gave us an answer. They did not want to tell us it was air that was being obstructed. We felt like visitors at the Olympiad; the next contender was Parkinson's disease. The competition to take him out was fierce, and age entered the contest as well.

Somehow, the attitude of this man enabled him to live his life the best he could without being a victim.

"Evie, those are conditions of life. They do not define who I am. No disease can do that unless I choose to give power where there is none. Would you please read what you wrote? I am listening."

"Donald, before I start, I must thank you for all that you are. One remarkable human you are! As soon as I come up with better words I will let you know. For now, take remarkable."

I was close to him, with a kiss and a hug he gave me the signal to read on. I reminded him again of my accent when I read, but he had grown accustomed to it, so I read.

"There was an event on a particular cold December night in 1928, a primal and amorous stirring followed by a release. A crack through the hundred-year-old wood-framed window allowed the northern winds to hum a triumphant tune of life. The resonances of everything original, ancient and primal could be heard, but no one talked about these things. Soon other noises took on their own voices. A law established long before that night brought something else in to play. No room for concern or fear on that cold night, the echoes of humanity fulfilling itself was enough.

"Under the cover of darkness, and to be remembered a while, mystery and submission gave way to a moment of bliss. Soon enough it was daybreak and time again to face the reality of a life in poverty. Nature, however, had plans and an outcome in mind.

"There was a long intermission, some confusion, and a period of limbo followed what was incomprehensible. A tunnel opening a gate revealed moist walls. No darkness had appeared so sinister, yet it was the way.

"Because life demanded it, a moment that felt like an eternity was followed by a sense of awareness. The presence of fear gave way to a victorious determination for survival. The combative struggle subsided, another form took place, and that took more than 280 days of pure determination. A mission had to be accomplished.

"Finally the time to enter life had arrived. The tunnel once visited in one form showed it's *opening* and once more it was time for something else to begin. Since the dawn of mankind it had been this way."

I paused and looked at him. He was smiling while I was making attempts at describing the marvels of the preconception process when only one privileged visitor, complete with a tail, would be anointed. Over a hundred million sperm would not enter the chamber where life itself would begin.

It was apparent, between silence and prose, there were mysteries to be discovered, to smile about or to ponder. He continued to observe me. He had a pleasant but enigmatic smile. Again, he gave me the signal to continue.

"Boom, boom-boom, boom, a predisposed and sometimes not perfect rhythm from a master's baton took over. The primal thump of a heart was soon audible, and a circle of events had to come to fruition. Nourished and protected, a new being was to visit an unknown world. A rendez-vous had to be kept for that was the way.

"Hostile air had to fill lungs never before used. A cry for help followed this frightening feeling. Boom, boom boom, boom. That was the rhythm, and this would be the way of life, until the master's baton would stop the orchestra."

Again, I looked at him. In his eyes I saw wetness. I stopped. In my eyes were free flowing tears. I approached him. My head on his shoulder, one hand on his chest, had become my favorite place to be. It was handy, he then could massage at least one shoulder and my head. I enjoyed that and so did he.

We talked a bit about the processes of pre and post birth. For us, it was all speculations since forces unknown to us made sure we did not remember being born. It was the beginning of life's continuum we did not seem to muster. I made attempts to remember the passages of my own journey but could not. I asked him, and he too could not remember anything at all. We were not privileged to carry these memories with us.

He gave me the signal to continue.

"Back in the queen's chamber, the wet and dark walls of the tunnel had to open the doorway. A place full of noise, disappointments, joys and sorrows, and only one predictable outcome, and this work of a master's hand was called a *birth*.

"A doorway opened to allow the first expulsion to take place. There were no preparations for this event. Expressions of fear, trepidation and anxiety, mixed with a welcoming impression of paradise could be felt. I asked, could this transaction have been the metaphoric expulsion from the Garden of Eden spoken of in biblical stories? It was again a great unknown. On the day of a birth, none of this matters."

He patted my head, and with his left index finger made a circle on my forehead. It was his long-established way of giving me a benediction.

There was silence, and I fell asleep.

There was Space

It was two years after these series of encounters that this man and I decided to become husband and wife. A kinship of souls had risen, and the need to be together grew more pronounced. Having been married before, and also having experienced a variety of relationships, we did not call what we felt *love*. Perhaps it was a matter of not knowing the words to give to the feelings we were experiencing. For both of us there was something unspecified and foreign. We respected each other's autonomy and sense of freedom, which was something important to both of us.

I talked of marriage and, feeling being married more than once, I did not require or want a traditional wedding. Since we talked a great deal, he had told me numerous stories about the Grand Canyon, where he spent a fairly long time. He took my statement about the ridiculousness of a traditional marriage ceremony seriously. He suggested we be married in a particular spot he loved at the Grand Canyon.

Many times with friends and relatives I travelled to the South Rim to show the splendor of the Grand Canyon, but I had not been to the North Rim.

It was on a windy and brisk afternoon of September that the people who introduced us, ministers of a church we did not attend, officiated the Rim-side ceremony.

Let's Go For A Short Walk

I had no bouquet and decided to pick wild dried flowers on the edge of the Canyon. While I did that, the officiating minister explained to Donald, my husband-to-be, that a marriage ceremony needed two witnesses to become legal. The presiding minister was not a witness. The prenuptial challenge was solved when a bus arrived. Groups of people came down to see the view from Point Imperial: our assigned wedding cathedral. Don walked up to a couple and asked if they would agree to be witnesses to a marriage. Ten minutes later we were husband and wife.

We had both admired the work of Khalil Gibran, the poet from Lebanon, and decided to read excerpts from one of his poems:

"You shall be together even in the silent memory of God.

But let there be spaces in your togetherness,

And let the winds of the heavens dance between you.

Love one another, but make not a bond of love,

Let it rather be a moving sea between the shores of your souls.

Fill each other's cup but drink not from one cup.

Sing and dance together and be joyous

Let each one of you dance alone.

For the pillars of the temple stand apart."

We had our witnesses and the people from the bus were our guests. The minister's husband walked me the few steps to the edge of Point Imperial where two pine trees acted as the pillars of the temple. The conductor had found a ribbon left in his bus; he helped me tie my wedding bouquet. The dried wild flowers I picked were in shades of brown representing the earth to me, touches of orange and old rose reminded me of the age differences of our lives. The silk ribbon was brilliant red and managed to tie together what was to become sacred.

Our marriage began with all that was unusual, and carved out for us a slice of life we had not counted on.

It was during a grand excursion to the West that we met a group of indigenous people selling their wares. With them was a grandmother. She had a particularly kind face. She called us to her, asking what we were doing on Navajo land. We told her we had been married only a few days and decided to explore places we did not know. Don told her he had taken the wrong turn, and had not meant to intrude or trespass. She asked if we were thirsty. We were not. From a basket, she pulled a vessel with two spouts and she said: "This is a wedding vessel. You fill it full, but you each drink from a different spout." Along with this gift, she gave us directions back to the main road. We both talked about the symbolic implication of this vessel. We had chosen the poem from Gibran telling us to drink from separate cups. I felt hoisted to a place I did not know existed. Don asked me to explain my feelings to him, but since I had never experienced them before, I could not clarify what this burst of emotions was like.

We were silent again, travelling to a destination that would eventually reveal itself. I was thinking of the two spouts. We were indeed two individuals who did not drink from the same glass.

A relationship filled with conversations brought balance to our independent nature. Admiration and room for continual growth was a model that worked for us. The quality of this phase of my life still remains mysterious and sacred.

While some people talk of soul mates, we did not. It was a decade into our marriage when he told me that he felt we were twin flames of the soul. Perhaps we were that, yet we knew the individuality of our personal flames. Separately and consciously, we made efforts to illuminate whatever we could. As one beacon, we never forgot how to join our flames. This model became an integral part of our relationship.

The decision to walk side-by-side the distance our lives would take us was a choice we made of sober minds. We were not attached to illusions of outcomes. The idea was to take life as it was granted, to experience it fully as long as we could. When one fell or faltered, the other was there to assist to stand up again. Acceptance becomes a good guide to flavor our dance. Aware that all lives come with interruptions, sorrow, and joy, we became observers being observed.

Years later, I remembered something he said:

"Eveline, to explain life to myself I visualize a flower that knows it has to look up to the sun to open up, and once that is done, the contract is over. Sweetheart, all this happens within a *clock*, a distorted circle of time and life."

I was aware of the flower of life because I had studied some sacred geometry, but he was not talking about that. I understood looking up to the sun because I knew all life on this planet needed the sun. It took longer to realize the worth of his *circle of life, his clock*.

In our existences, we were granted opportunities and seasons to explore all that our lives had to offer. We soon became aware that not all people took these offerings seriously. For us, savoring life's gifts demanded that we also talk about the end-of-life contracts.

The Cave

I continue to be enthralled by the rhythm of our lives and how it all began.

Though the mountaintop of our first walk to the circle below us, was only a metaphor for as above so below, walking the labyrinth on my property often brought me the same feeling of awe.

Montezuma Well begged for its exploration. Together we began to walk down; the steps to the beginning of this excursion were precipitous.

I knew the secret place behind the well; a shaman had taken me there. For reasons I did not know, it was not open to the public. I took him there. The sacred, dark, heart-shaped rock was awaiting our arrival. To experience it, I got on my knees and allowed my third eye to rest on its shape. Like in a grotto from some far away, saintly place, water trickled to a natural canal. Donald stood to my left side. When I got up, he did the same thing and then we cupped our hands and drank this most limpid water.

Nothing needed to be said. We continued the walk.

Today I know this moment in our history was a gift from the universe. It was also the first time that with the thumb of his left hand he made a circle on my forehead.

Let's Go For A Short Walk

It was during that walk that Donald mentioned his idea of reality. His wish was to remember to live his life in the ever-present moment. He did this with an open heart. The greater idea, he said, was to learn to appreciate the gifts of awareness. His words resonated with me.

The man was a teacher, and we followed a guidance that needed no name. Soon enough, our lives became a series of adventures.

Our first, long walk did not bring us to the source of Montezuma Well. Perhaps we only had to learn what we needed to. There is solace in satisfaction and acceptance.

Our search could have been a preamble to visiting the well instead—The Well of Montezuma—a sacred place to many. We were in an environment to discuss the first inhabitants of the place, the indigenous people of the Americas. We chose instead to talk about our own development.

"Eveline, some say the surroundings of this well are known for altering the sagacity of discernment. You are lucky to reside close enough. I like the idea that you come here to sit on the upper rocks. Do you have a favorite rock, and have you gone in any of the caves?"

"Yes I do have a favorite rock, it likes my body, and it is right next to a juniper I can lean on. When I am there, I pick up dried leaves and pine needles, crush them to enhance the scent, and spread them around me. It is my ceremony to the ancestors. I have not been inside the cave."

"Eveline, I am sure the ancient spirits feel honored every time you come to the well. I bet the interior of the cave could use your kind of energy. You know, there's only one open anymore. I guess the others were not readily accessible and too dangerous. The first time I came here, the sky was overcast, yet I felt like a part of my soul went through an opening. This is where I began to examine my own consciousness. Every time I come here, I find a place to sit, and just think. It's magical. After a short while here I can change the things I need to. I can grow."

I turned a bit, and looked at him. I did not take the next step, but was balancing on one foot like a Navajo warrior during a dance to

Grandfather sun. All along our walk we talked about changes required to grow and become better people. Now I wondered how much he knew about the various indigenous tribes of the region. Our conversations were not about regional people, and my mind was occupied with the fact that I had never met a man who was courageous enough to admit not only to flaws but who also had a willingness to change them. Puzzled as I was, I eventually took another step thinking most people did not talk about drastic and self-directed changes in their lives. I know I did not.

My preference was to brush off or hide the things I did not like about myself. For him, I surmised, it was about learning new behaviors, with the promise of developing a nobler personality.

I was talking, walking, observing, and my mind was going faster than I could catch the thoughts that were coming at me like a tornado. I recalled my mother telling me this was the reason Persian Rugs were woven! *One puts dirty laundry under the rug!* I know she was serious about her pronouncement. I could not help but think of my mother, and her numerous rugs.

This man was the opposite of all that I knew. He had accomplished his mission to change himself in order to like who he was. I was awed by this remarkable accomplishment. I knew I could learn about being a better person by simply watching him.

We walked on toward a place I did not know. The steps he took did not seem tentative. The ones I took felt as if I was at the edge of an abyss. For dear life I held onto his hand.

"You have good balance. You stayed on one foot quite a while. You will have to show me what Yoga practices gave you such equilibrium. Look, do you see this rock, to the right of that arch? Why don't you sit a moment? This is the entrance to the cave I was talking to you about."

I was tired of walking up and down the sides of the well and looking into cliff dwellings we could not enter. I knew these ruins had not felt anyone's footprints for a long time. Resting a while was a good idea. I wondered about the person smart enough to place the flat rock where it was, exactly where it needed to be. I sat, and one more time, looked up at this well groomed man. Distinctively, a man comfortable with all that he was. There was a kind of inner confidence about him.

"You see, Eveline, the universe does not ask for much. I believe that we are the universe, and we have been around a long time. We know what we need to know.

"Most of us forget what we knew, that's all. The pompous importance we give ourselves has no significance unless it is to feed our ego. If we don't know how to appreciate who we are, our names and fortunes are not very important.

"I have come to believe that the universe does not ask us to pray or go to any church or temple to find what is within each of us. It took me a long time to realize and accept this. You have no idea how much I had to search for what was inside. Let's see, how I can put it? Once I discovered who I was, many things unwanted or not needed dropped off. Changing the things I did not like about myself became a byproduct of practicing some compassion about my fellow men, but especially myself. I had to learn to love *me*. Change does not happen overnight. I also had to forgive myself for all the things I judged were wrong with me. I didn't know they were part of lessons I was learning. The *me* that you met is the version I worked on for a long while. Great people assisted me in becoming who I am today.

"I found this place a long time ago when I was learning to be alone. I think I must have been here at least a hundred times. I am surprised I never ran into you. Here in this ancient incubator, if I can call it that, I found the safety to think and start to initiate the changes I needed to make in my life. Eveline, all the times that I came here I never met a person inside. I know now, I never met *you* here because I was not ready. We were supposed to be involved in our own self-discovery.

"Eveline, to change anything in life we must first accept the idea that change is necessary. The changes themselves can be difficult, but I think once acceptance comes into the picture, strength grows. I had to change friends, and for sure behavior—I had to stop drinking. The darkness of this cave gave light to my soul. Many things about who we are can be discovered in such places. I guess this is similar to what you did in the sweat lodge or the vision quest you talked about. Remember, one of these days, you must tell me about that."

He took my hand, and I got up without resistance. It was time to enter the cave with the low opening. Once inside, with a slight turn, nothing was visible. There was not a glimmer of light and if there was a passage to escape, it could not be seen. The breeze of moments ago gave way to a scent of burned sage. We were in a subterranean place, a real cave, and while this man was comfortable, I was not. I had never been inside a cave. My closet was the only cave I ever ventured into.

The steps he took were not hesitant. Mine were. I held onto his hand.

"Because of this place, I resolved to make changes in behavior. My true character emerged. Eveline, today, I like who I am, and no one can take that away from me."

I responded with a smile he could not see. I too had been in a place to face fears and demons. I said nothing. He continued to talk.

"Eveline, I heard that this area was a place occupied by the Sin Agua Indians during pre-Columbian times. First, they were not called Indian, and Sin Agua in Spanish means *"without water"*. Whoever gave this name to the tribe, did not know about the well. There is plenty of water and I think some fish too. I must say the place that gave me so much did not give me the tools to learn more about it. At that time, my interest was the solitude I needed, and what I was learning about me. I am not an archeologist nor a fisherman, so I left such discoveries to others."

As he spoke, I could only imagine the time, discipline, and the persistence it must have taken to arrive at the place of changes? He had released my hand and I took a few more steps to go deeper into the womb of the earth. Discovering that he was a man of courage and noble character gave me a sense of acceptance toward another human being. A sort of magic allowed me to vacate my usual mode. I was not exactly comfortable in the great unknown of this chamber, but at ease with him and also myself I could explore what I was feeling. Like many proceedings in life, in no time, I imagined the walls falling on us. One turn of the head, and a new perspective emerged. Knowing we were to die at one point or another became the acceptable method to understand the experience, inside this cave. By a phenomenon I did not count on, I had released the last vestige of fear I had.

The visit to the cave united more than our hands. The energy between us was both palpable, and foreign to me.

Today as I write these words, I smile again because the messages from this man were delivered with stories and subtle teachings sandwiched within.

"Donald, I want to know how you did this—coming to this place could not have been enough. Changing behavior is never easy and yet, you give me the impression of a relatively painless march toward self-reckoning. Perhaps you can teach me the secret. Though I tell my children that I am perfect, I know there is room for a lot of improvement.

"The sweat lodges that I attend open the space for me to learn a great deal about myself. You do understand, a sweat lodge is exactly that, a place where you sweat to release what has encumbered your majesty. You sit on the ground in a small confined place, a circle. In the center next to your feet are rocks that have been in a raging fire all day long. They provide extreme heat. I have no idea what the temperature is inside, but I have experienced a thin layer of skin peeling off. In other words, you get to cook yourself. The medicine man knows what can and cannot be tolerated. No one gets hurt unless some want-to-be Indian pretends to be a shaman. These folks know nothing about sweat lodges and some accidents have happened due to ignorance of the imposters. The idea is to transcend what is so uncomfortable, and find a center within where all is calm and not hot. I think this is where I started to count seriously. One, two, three, four, breathe in. One, two, three, four, hold the breath, one more set of four and breathe out. I have not a clue how many times I went through this count in the lodge. When I found that place in the center of all that I was, I felt I had arrived. Today, I can say, I am constantly in a state of arriving. By the way, what I did was similar to yoga breathing—the count is different, the end result about the same.

"Don, I have not walked where you are, and my spirit is slow to learn the subtleties. I am to go on a vision quest but the date has not been set. Do you know anything about that? Though I have not gone, I have a feeling this cave could be a close comparative. What possessed you to go inside the cave anyway?"

"Eveline, probably something akin to your need to go inside a sweat lodge. I think all aware human beings come to a state in their lives where there is a requirement to be sufficiently vulnerable for changes to occur. That need could come from following inner guidance or some other motivator. I believe it is different for each person.

"First things first. Whatever you do in life, Eveline, you must start where you are. I am certain you know that. In my case, it was a process. I encountered some difficulties and had to look at myself. Most of us want everything to be perfect, and fast, but we are afraid of changing anything. We don't like to be uncomfortable in our own skin. I believe this is something unspoken of that scares all people.

"Well, Donald, I believe you are correct. Any new venture in my life begins from where I stand, be it figuratively or otherwise. I am adventuresome, but I know how to think and conduct myself not to get hurt too often. I am not prone to making abrupt decisions, yet if something feels right, I could appear to be impulsive. This attitude could be the advantage of following my own guidance or being a singular person. By the way *singular* is the expression my brother uses to describe my character. With siblings decades older than I am, I learned to be comfortable with myself. Like you, I noticed, I answer only to myself. By the time I could talk, I had no siblings around. They were married and/or away at college somewhere. I was home-schooled, so being a singular person was all I could be. I like the contentment I find with myself."

"Eveline, having observed you some, I think you don't have any problems making up your mind about anything. You are pretty fearless.

Anyway, as for this cave, I like places like this. I found it when I was walking around. It was a time in my life for change. I think the guidance you talk about worked for me also. I discovered the entrance, and without thinking about dangers or anything else, I entered. Something profound that I am not sure I can explain happened to me that day. I was not comfortable with the darkness, but deep in my soul, with an empty hole in place of a heart, I felt I needed to stay a while. I took some steps and my foot hit something. Like a blind man would hit an object, I examined what it was with my hands—a stone. The top surface felt smooth, the sides were not. I could not tell what it was doing there or what it was. It was about the same height all over. I decided it was a bench for me to use. I sat on it, and I even lay down a while. It came to me the bench was not a bench. I had heard of birthing places that indigenous people used. I decided it was a place where women gave birth. Don't ask me why this came to mind.

"Eveline, the next time I came I brought a flashlight. Remember we bent way down to enter, once inside with light, I could see this room has a ceiling at least nine feet high. The space is an easy twenty feet long by at least eighteen wide. It's a cave, so nothing is smooth or straight. Only the bench has a smooth surface. At one end I could see where there had been fire, but I could not tell if the soot was from ancient or new smoke. I wondered where the smoke went out. I didn't see a hole. I did not stop to think about any of this.

"Eveline, whatever brought me here, I needed to understand what was going on within. The experience of checking surfaces with my hands and not my eyes gave me an understanding of how a blind person felt. I suddenly did not take my vision for granted. I thought about that for a long time. I became aware that I had neglected the being that I was, taking everything in life for granted as if I was going to live forever. My mind grew open in this place, and other events and people were with me to usher my growth."

"Donald, it is obvious to me, you follow some kind of guidance, and by so doing you acquired knowledge and wisdom. Nice! I am glad we met."

Revelation in a Cave

"Eveline, it never occurred to me that I would bring anyone to this space, and if I did, I would not be talking about myself. I now recognize when you and I opened ourselves up, life as we narrowly understood it, put on a feast for us. I am getting a better interpretation of my own being. I am not my body. This cave provided me with an understanding of my ego. As my life happens, the experiences are felt through my body, but my soul is what holds me accountable. Am I making sense to you?

"Yes, absolutely, you are making sense."

"Eveline, I can tell you, this is when I began to accept some guidance from within. Up to that time I was pretty unconscious. What puzzles me the most is how I managed to follow intuition I did not know existed or that I was capable of obeying."

"Donald, I can tell you this is similar to the way I think. I did not study religions as you have, but somehow, I know I am a lot more than my body. Do not get me wrong, I take care of that body; I love it; I take it seriously; I am very vain and perhaps this is why I am a vegetarian. I also know to use that body well for the transport of my soul because as you just said, the soul experiences what our body feels. With all this, I cannot even explain what my soul is. I know if there is such a thing, it is more than what I think I am. So yes, again, you are making perfect sense."

"Eveline, my hope is to have open-minded people around me who are able to venture into such discussions. Are those the type of conversations you have when you go to home of the Mother of Holistic Medicine? I want to know more about that too. I met Dr. Gladys McGarey a couple of times. I believe the fact that she was born in India gave her that holistic edge on life. You are lucky to know her."

"Donald, Dr. Gladys is a spectacular woman of knowledge. At her home we discuss the Edgar Cayce material. He is known as the sleeping prophet. We read one or two paragraphs from a book. We then spend three hours talking about our understanding of what we read. We discuss how our lives are affected by what we experience from the reading, or better yet, what we digest from it. I think overall, I can say we talk about guidance."

"I can say God, as I understand it, got me to this cave. I know about the Cayce material. Now I can tell you more. Somewhere in the darkness, I learned with difficulty to accept the way my life was unfolding. I made it here at a time when I was devastated. A divorce robbed me of my wife. I had no one to take to parties and show off. Pathetic, I know, but this was the truth at that time. I denied the idea that I was responsible for what went on in my marriage. I was also ashamed because I could not even keep a wife. Desperation and hopelessness took no time to invade every minute of my life. Sitting on that rock, I realized I never treated my wife as an individual. I don't know where I got the idea that I had to oversee and control her life. She was my wife, my possession. Who knows, maybe she did not want that? I don't know. I never asked how she felt about anything. She, on the other hand, was not a communicator.

"Empty, despondent, and ashamed—I drank some more. I was Irish, and that was my excuse. Life gave me a good trashing because of my behavior. The possibilities for changes were always there, but my ego got in the way.

"Forgive me, dear, I am talking a lot. Thank you for listening. I am like the seeds you plant in your garden. You water them. They grow. You gave me the opportunity to speak and I did."

"Donald, I am glad you felt at ease to talk openly. What you said you discovered about *yourself* gave me the opportunity to learn a great deal about you. I do not understand the dynamics of excessive drinking. You said you had a need to control your wife, yet you could not control your life. Would you kindly explain this to me?"

"I can only explain what I experienced. In counseling of others, I applied what skill and knowledge I acquired from schools. I used my own life to make valid points. It is not easy to explain the cycles of any existence or why life seems to present itself in cycles. You say karma, I say destiny, yet I can't prove either."

We talked a long while in the darkness of the cave. Eventually my eyes regained clear vision. A sense of calm permeated this womb. I was in a somewhat circular cave. He must have sensed my discovery because he continued to talk as if I had given him a signal.

"If you decide to return here, quiet yourself before you enter the cave. If you can, leave your fears outside. Once you do this, a new world opens up to you. The best thing is to have no expectations and try to visualize the circle that envelops you. I envision it as a clock. I don't know what works for all people, but this continually works for me. Every time I come here, a new window is opened and creates a vista for more self-discovery. In my mind, I place my growth at different times in my imaginary clock."

In a non-assuming way he radiated confidence. I liked that about him. He knew who he was. He revealed only what was important to him. He had strength of character.

"Eveline, I suspect the time will come soon when I will tell you more about myself. I'm only getting to know you.

"I can tell you, I am an active participant in my life. As we develop our friendship I would like to explore this dimension of who I am with you. It is my hope that you too will share your development with me. We seem to be compatible that way. I already know you are a private person. Sorry I forgot, you or your brother called it singular. I also know you observe everything around you. Yet I see something wide open about you.

"We both know that life itself is about change, and I have a feeling you recognize this in yourself. By the way, I haven't ever taken anyone to this cave."

We were silent a while.

"Donald, I understand some of the changes in your life. Now I must ask, why did you bring me here? I could have been a brittle, insecure person who could have fallen apart at the darkness of this place."

"Eveline, it took me three seconds or less to know there was nothing fragile about you."

"You are right. I agree I am not the delicate or fragile type. Life did not grant me these sorts of options. I can tell you, I would have gotten used to that in a hurry. Moments ago you talked of a clock that you live by. Would you please explain your concept to me? When you talk of the clock, are you referring to the idea of a circle, a time continuum, or some reference to numbers and times of life? I am not understanding."

"It's all of the above because no matter what you are doing, you must begin where you are. This is the clock part. By now you know I talk a lot. I was attempting to explain to you that when I want to make changes in my life there is no need for stalling or analyzing; I know what needs to be changed. I procrastinated a long time. That's because I was afraid. So, now when I am engaged in any new enterprise, I begin where I am in that imaginary clock.

"I would like to explore my clock idea later. The subject of a clock will take time. To explore the movements of my life, I had first to recognize everything that happens has a time and a reason. In other words, life has time, seasons and reasons.

"I enjoyed taking to you, it's getting dark outside. I must get you home. The park ranger will be closing the gate soon."

Obscurities in Dialogue

My and Don's lives, filled with conversations, could also be packed with inferences and complete stops. Between the two, I found his wisdom. This day, as I was reading about my perception of events relating to his birth, his mind took a side trip. He had too many stories to tell me, and too much wisdom to bring forth. He looked at me with a puzzled grin. The serious air of a patriarch showed between his brows. He held his staff with his left hand, sat up and took over.

"Evie, I think your articulations of a birth are fascinating. This brings me to something else.

"I feel in any life, and certainly my life, the choices we make between life and death are events with meaning. The rest is all conjectures. Evie, you know about perceptions and opinions. We have those, and we scream them out, too often forgetting they are about the lessons given to us to grow from. There are other times when we develop what we think is our own perception or opinion, yet, we're merely followers of some other person's ideology. This is one reason I could not stick to any given religion or political party.

"As far as I know, it is from our slow human development that we acquire our ideals—the stuff that guides our every move. We look at things differently every time we grow a little. I think, if we take the time to develop ideals to live by, they do not change. Only ideas change. All this is about experiences that provide us with wisdom. We may change our minds and create new ideas, and have all kinds of conflicts to resolve, but to be a well, integrated person we must remain true to our ideals. The odd thing is that whatever our actions, most times, we come to our senses and get back on track. That is following and being cognizant of our personal ideal."

I called Don My Patriarch and when he spoke with me, his words not only resonated, but often they penetrated my core. Most often I was a student of great minds. Destiny, or pure luck, made me grateful. I had no need to know why a gift was given to me. My task was to enjoy it.

"Evie, while we are constantly attempting to change the world around us, we don't take ourselves seriously enough to change our behavior or what we need to know in order to function and to become better than we were moments ago. We are a society that wants instant gratification. My sister told me a thousand times I got drunk to get the gratification she talked about, but I could never get there. I can tell you, there are no such things as mistakes. There is always a lesson to learn."

"So, what is that lesson you needed to learn?"

"Evie, it does not work like that. I have my lessons to learn and you have yours. We can't allow ourselves to be influenced by how other people think. We can't influence one another either."

He expressed thoughts that touched me deeply.

The delivery of his wisdom often needed integration and assimilation. I needed time to digest.

"Evie, when you need time to assimilate anything, give yourself permission to take the time that you need. I am going to take a nap."

When he woke up, he went back to talk about my birthing ideas. We speculated at length about this passage to and out of the womb. We wondered why it was not consciously felt or remembered.

He decided that I must have remembered something about my birth. How else could I write about it? My husband may have been a wise man, but he had no idea about the workings of the human body. He joined me as I laughed about the anatomy lessons he never had.

Since anatomy was not his strong suit and he preferred philosophy, we jumped to another subject. *How did one arrive at the decision to enter this unknown world with the parents we chose, and why? Was it all predestined?*

For hours we discussed the possible reasons, all to no avail. I wanted to know what destiny was. No one had ever told me. We talked about cosmic events, spontaneous or otherwise. We never came up with a satisfactory answer.

"Don, do you think we are alive because we are part of some godly energy with a sense of humor? Why do we have experiences we cannot explain?"

Our conversations and searches became ours to savor. Most were entertaining, and were avenues to escape looking at death in the eyes. Our relationship made those private moments we held reverent.

"Evie, based on how I believe the world operates, I have a feeling we are given these thoughts to learn from. We are in a large classroom and the courses to take are many."

Somewhere along the way, we had done a good job of accepting the things we could not change. Our mental gymnastics became exciting and entertaining. We enjoyed each other's minds.

"I agree with you, Evie. To some degree, we do well with a bunch of unknowns. My entire life, however, I have questioned the very fiber of my existence. Here I am, eighty-five years old, and I do not have the answer.

"Since *you* have the energy and the desire, I'll watch you as you explore *your* life."

My interest was to discover what controlled universal time. I felt the clock he often talked about had something to do with that control system. Unlike Einstein, I could not articulate my feelings though I made many attempts. I was on the other side of science. I came to accept that my nature was not based on tangible knowledge. Any tunnel I went through was not always filled with light but I always came out knowing more than I did when I entered it. I suppose it is safe to say, I was to find new beginnings. As usual, my head was full of questions. Don, on the other hand, made attempts to unravel what I could not. He had reached a point of wisdom in his life that permitted him to be more accepting and less questioning.

He told me about the grand cycles of life. The cycles, he understood well. He also told me about the subjective activities we put ourselves into. Was he trying to tell me I was responsible for the various jams, mistakes and misadventures I embraced of my own volition as part of the journey I took?

"Don, you often splinter my illusions."

Those were considerations we gave to our mundane life. Taking as much time as we deemed necessary, we lived a momentous life of our making.

A body cloaked in many diseases left his mind to contain many freedoms.

He was fascinated by the work of Michelangelo. If this man regretted anything at all, it was not having allowed himself to visit the Sistine Chapel. He was knowledgeable about the artist's entire body of work. I found this fascinating, since art was not necessarily one of the strong essentials of his life. We were talking about Michelangelo's David when he changed the conversation and talked about Pope Julius II.

Raised a Roman Catholic, and as odd as it may sound, this religious condition dedicated that one day Don would be a priest. He knew all sorts of stories about the religion and the people around it. I knew none. He told me of conversations between artist and pope. They too had a fascination about the beginning and the end of life. I, on the other hand, did not think popes or other men of the cloth explored more than heaven. I wondered if they knew about the existence of the Tibetan Book of the Dead, which we had read more than once. Don found this book fascinating and far from Christian canon. We explored books in order to know better how to live from the soul. Lao Tzu was a philosopher he paid great attention to.

It was during our endless conversations that we both questioned if Michelangelo and Pope Julius II wanted the same things we did? We knew living everyday life from soul and spirit was not easy. The demands of our quotidian life were rigorous and travelled in many directions. I wondered if, for a pope or an artist, life's many questions were any different.

Some of our best and deepest conversations were often left open to further speculations.

I was homeschooled and no one talked about religion to me. One of my aunts was a pretty fervent Catholic. She made angel wings for girls to wear during some Catholic holidays. Having ancestry embracing more than one religion, I found myself accepting all religions. My name is of French Jewish lineage. Among family members we often made fun of the shape of our noses. That was religious enough for us. From my mother's people of Spain, I understood the influence of the Muslim occupation of Andalusia for seven hundred years. I must say, I am liberated from religious rule.

As always, our conversations continued to jump subjects. We would drop one and catch the other midstream. The Last Judgment behind the altar wall of the Sistine Chapel became the next object of our deliberations. I had seen it as a magnificent piece of art, but never questioned why bare of status and ranks, the figures were naked to face their maker. Don told me Pope Julius II never got to see the finished project. He was dead before it was finished. In my head, still full of questions, I wondered if this great painter, sculptor, poet had given the viewing audience his explanation of matters of life and death? After all, at death, our spirits or souls are naked, without the cover of our bodies. What was this artist telling us?

Let's Go For A Short Walk

Like the naked truth we were facing, we did not know the answer to the reason why this painter had chosen the naked figures for his painting.

Our sedentary life, like the movement of the winds, brought passion to our discussions. Emotions and intellect were always well nourished.

I was immersed in thoughts of the Sistine Chapel when I noticed the transparency of the soul in the eyes looking at me. Don's philosopher's brows enhanced his facial bones. In his eyes I saw the many gifts I received to inspire my own visions.

Every day it became more obvious; Don and I had conversations travelling distances and dimensions. One day on the ever-present yellow pad at his side, Don made a circle and a dot. He looked at me as if I was to guess the meaning of his drawing. It was not the Perfect Circle of Giotto di Bondone. An artist Don was not. He felt this circle was Michelangelo's greatest discovery. As often before, I was confused. Michelangelo was not known for a circle and a dot. I felt certain, this man who was able to point me to the direction of light and clarity, had lost his mind. Ultimately all I knew was a circle had great meaning in Don's life. He referred to circles often.

Often enough Don spoke of the cycle of his life and of clocks. He even gave me a watch, which was missing hands. I never asked what I was to do with this circle of numbers and no hands. He was not a man who jumped to conclusions, nor did he latch onto anything without a reason. I simply did not know his reasons. The day he gave me his watch, with the band made by an indigenous artist. He told me I would know what to do with it. He said he could see it around my neck. I was convinced he often found pleasure in my puzzled eyes. How would I wear a watchband around my neck? This man left me baffled often. Somehow, always, I would come across a suitable explanation.

It was over a year after he died, with the help of the man who created our wedding bands, that the answer was revealed. I showed him the watch. He took it. He also took the wedding bands, and told me he would think. Christopher and I had been friends for many decades. I trusted he would create something I would like. He did just that.

Like most times the conversations between Don and myself, however interesting, had to adapt to the limited capacity of his lungs.

"One day soon, I will continue this conversation. Why don't you finish reading what you wrote? Get me some oxygen first. Evie, having lungs that don't work the way they were meant to is hard to cope with. I am glad I never smoked or had lung cancer. Having COPD is hard enough. Chronic Obstructive Pulmonary Disease, they could have come up with some other name.

"We will talk about the circle and what it means to me. Evie, you must realize everything discovered in a lifetime has meaning.

"Don't take my words. Discover for yourself. I can only point you toward what I learned along the way. By the way, my dear, you do that well."

Before continuing the conversation, a breathing treatment had to be administered. It was important that I stop and muse about life's many conditions.

Let Us Continue About Birth

After a good nap, he did not wish to talk about circles or churches. He was restored, and wanted me to continue. I began to read, but first, reminded him that this time I would be talking about his mother giving birth to him. The look on his face was one of subtle horror. I had to remind him that women had been having babies long before his mother.

He laughed, letting me know he was somewhat aware. We found humor where it hid from us.

I began to read where I believed I had stopped.

"There was a great deal of movement throughout the walls of a habitat tranquil for over nine months. The child felt he was being pushed downward to a place he did not know. Calm returned every so often, there was also a sense of caresses, and the pushing downward would start all over again. None of this was familiar. This episode was both pleasing, but also frightening. He could not make the movements stop. He had to give in. A universal agreement signed—without his knowledge—took precedence.

"Suddenly, the wetness and safety of the dark chamber became a tunnel, and without announcement, it gave way to a gust of wind.

Fighting for survival had to take over, that too was a law—a law of things primal.

"This episode happened without notable fanfare. The birth was that of a boy they named Donald Thomas Dailey. The date was the sixteenth day of September in the year 1929. The place called Utica, in the state of New York, gave this healthy baby boy a place in history."

I stopped a moment to judge his impression. Behind the well groomed beard and mustache he was pensive, and he smiled. He gave me the sign to go on. I could see moisture in his eyes, and soon behind a controlled flow of tears something bright opened up for me to appreciate. He called me closer to him. He gave me a hug. He took the oxygen mask off.

"Evie, you give my existence reason for being. I wish I could reciprocate."

"Don, your hugs show me understanding when I go berserk, acceptance when I foul up, affection and love that I cannot even explain, all give my life reason for being. You give, and you reciprocate hundreds of times."

"Evie, providence has brought us oneness that was not always in our lives. That makes us fortunate people. I think most of us humans forget that we are born neutral. We make choices to exclude, to fear what we do not understand or what is different than what we are. Take the two of us. We are not the same. We made the conscious choice to learn from each other, to accept each other. It is in the choice of acceptance that we can grow.

"Evie, I do know that choices, no matter how terrifying, must be made if we wish to become better human beings. Changes in lives must be made and accepted. The fact is, we all must learn to change and care for people: those close to us, and those far away. I am not saying it's easy. I think I did that as often as I could. When I found someone less fortunate than me and I was able to help, I did. Such actions did not make me a great person, but they made me feel good about myself.

"Do you remember when we went to serve people at the shelter? The few times we did this, I felt great. I know the people also felt as I did, because you served them. Thank you, Evie, you exposed me to so many different people. Did you know at first I was not comfortable? Now I realized your friends I labeled odd are all very great and intelligent people. To have wonderful and creative friends makes you a very special person. I am grateful for that.

"In my present condition, I find myself able to focus better. There are a lot fewer distractions. At the abbey, one of the senior abbots once told me he could tell from my eyes that I had trouble with my wondering mind. He was right, but once I learned to meditate, I could stop my mind from deliberating about things I couldn't change. You know I still do that. Did you know the monks at the abbey took a vow of silence? They could talk about an hour a day. During my stay there, I tried to find the one I wanted to talk to, and in the great hall I would sit next to him. There was always something important I needed to hear.

"The idea is we all need to be willing to receive what is being said."

"Dailey, are you telling me all these stories because you do not wish to hear about your birth?"

"No, you know I talk too much, it's ok to stop me you know! Go on, read."

"No oracle or astrologer predicted anything about this birth. When people are poor, they do not talk of changes or hope very much. The concerns they have are more immediate. In the case of your family, they never could fathom leaving or changing their station in life. This happens often when the mind is as poor as the bank account, if there is one. The idea of changing their lives would be an undertaking that would present insurmountable difficulties. At a young age, you, a child of Irish roots, were dedicated to the church: the Roman Catholic Church. This was the way of your mother's people. The priesthood presented to her the only chance her son had of leaving the life he was born into."

I was done with this part of my writing. My husband looked at me with the tenderness only he could display. As many times before, we connected without a word. Our eyes received the communion most people search for. Free flowing tears of gratitude for moments we shared added the final punctuation mark to what I had written and just read to him.

The New Baby Comes Home

"Evie, since you began my story at conception, I might as well tell you what I know about the first part of my life. It's all hearsay from my sisters who were old enough to remember. They told me the things my parents never talked about. I can only imagine how difficult it must have been for them not being able to provide for their children. I only remember a quiet, perhaps desperate kind of harmony between my mother and father. I suspect they did a lot of genuflecting in prayer for a better lot for their children and themselves. I suppose they had to pray for acceptance for the poverty they lived with.

"We both know that I came from a world very different from yours. For one, we didn't have servants, no gardener and certainly no chauffeur. We didn't have a car. Come to think of it, I don't think my father knew how to drive, and for sure my mother did not know.

"I once took her on a ride in a new Mercedes I purchased—a wing tip— she was not particularly impressed. I drove at 100 miles per hour and she did not flinch. When I stopped at a restaurant she was more impressed with the size of the piece of pie she had than the size of my engine. Funny the things I remember!

"Anyway, I was born in a Catholic hospital, Saint something, of course. Right now, I don't know that I ever knew the name. My sisters

Irene and Catherine were not allowed to visit me. Everything was different in 1929. Only at birth or when sick did children end up in hospitals. In Catholic churches or hospitals there were rules everyone had to obey. My sister Irene told me our father took them on a bus. At the stop in front of the hospital they got off and waited. My father went across to the hospital. A while later a nurse held me by a window on the second floor. I can only imagine what I looked like to them.

"The poverty my parents suffered was chronic. If I understand the stories I heard, I would say they were afraid to hope. They did not know how to attempt something different unless it was given to them. Eveline, I understand the dynamic of poverty. Most times those who are poor have no options. My parents never talked about being poor.

"My sisters told me when my mother went into labor, my parents had to take a bus that crossed the town to get to the hospital. A taxi would not have been an option. Seven days after my birth, the same bus took them back home. I also heard the bus driver who was a man with a job, told my parents they did not have to pay for the ride. As I reflect on all this, it is safe to say, people were different then.

"There was no money to buy clothes or anything for a new child. Before I came home, the Catholic Services prepared a bundle of clothes for a boy; they did a lot of charity that way. I learned years before my birth my father had injured a leg moving a piano. The few pennies he made that day were not enough to go to a hospital or a doctor. After that accident, he developed a limp. His left leg was never the same again. He never talked about pain, but I can imagine he must have suffered plenty. Receiving the clothes at the Catholic Services, my father walked three miles each way. By the time I came home I had whatever a baby boy needed.

"Eveline, few people know about the lives of their parents. I know these things because my sisters told me. My children do not know about these things.

"You see, my parents had no money for clothes for a new baby boy, the girl clothes left from my sisters were old and torn to shreds.

My mother used them as rags to clean the house. She also used the rags to clean other people's houses when she could get a job. She was an industrious woman.

"Evie, I can only picture, their first son, and no clothes for him. Mine was not a princely story. I am sure it must have been a devastating event for my parents. My sister Irene told me that everything changed when I got home. She and Catherine shared a bed, but there was no bed for me. The first three months I slept with my parents. The problem of space for me was resolved when someone gave my mother a small mattress. The lack of a crib was resolved with ingenuity. Every night after super, the table was cleared, the mattress—placed on top of it—that became my bed. So I would not fall, the table was pushed against a corner and chairs barricaded the other sides.

"If I understand correctly, my sisters took turns changing me and taking care of me when my mother was sewing for people. She also washed and ironed clothes for those who could afford to pay her. My sisters made sure to tell me they also helped when my mother was cooking for the family.

"I have come to believe because of the circumstances of our lives, we were a close knit bunch. We had no toys, and sometimes I feel we invented conversation. I still suffer from this affliction. The library gave us a window to view and read about the world.

"Not much later in my infancy, the mattress on the table became unsafe. The mattress was put under the table. I recall sleeping there, on the floor, on the small mattress. I was about three or so. I have no memories before three.

"I remember my mother telling me that I was a prince. I had my own fort under the kitchen table. That poor woman made sure I was not traumatized because of my sleeping arrangement. She also always had books from the library for me to look at. I was about four when she was able to teach me how to read. She had rigged a hanging bulb to get me light without disturbing the girls. The wire from the lamp dangled from a crack on the table. I suppose I could call it a swag lamp. I could turn the pages and look at pictures when everyone else was sleeping.

"I am glad you are a reader. It would be difficult if in the middle of the night I had to go in another room to read. We are a good pair, Evie.

"I became an avid reader and that never left me. She made sure that I always had a book with me. She was a good teacher. I knew the alphabet and she was teaching me how to sound out words by the time was just four. My mother imparted some good habits to me. You already know I held her in a special place in my heart. She still is, and often you do some things that remind me of her.

"You know what's interesting? If parents don't tell their kids they are poor, the kids don't develop the complexes attached to poverty. I didn't know we were poor. I can tell you, this changed when I went to school. Our clothes were from the church's exchange. I heard in the basement, they had a special room for the used clothes. My mother made sure that her children always wore clean and always pressed clothes. Maybe this is why my clothes today are always clean and pressed. We wore brown coats that were given by some organization. Kids with other color coats knew we were poor and they made fun of us.

"Evie, it's not only blacks that suffered from prejudice. Italians did and so did the Irish. Italians did not like Irish and it all went on because people thought they were supposed to hate anyone who was different from them. What is almost funny, but it's not: they all believed in a loving God. It took a long time for me to know we are all programmed early in life.

"I somehow became friends with most of the kids, the poor ones of course, except the Protestants. See, prejudice about religion has always existed. Today, we hate the Muslims. I was the smallest kid in the area, so my big friends looked out for me. In my neighborhood, the poor kids stuck together. The rich kids had nothing to do with the poor ones. Not much has changed. I don't know who the Protestant kids played with. They were poor. I knew because they too wore brown coats in the winter. Their families came from England, I think. They were not Catholics, and that was enough for my mom. I smile now because I know in her heart my mother did not know she was teaching me her prejudice. This is a universal failure in parenting."

To think of the level of poverty my husband came from often brought me tears. I took notes and sometimes the paper was very wet.

"My Italian friend Gino often invited me to eat with him. His mother liked me even though I was Irish. Gino was an only child. He was polite. I grew to love the Italian food the grandmother cooked. She did not speak English, but her food was great. One day, they gave me a bowl to take home. It was spaghetti and meatballs. My parents and sisters would not eat the strange foods with a red sauce and stringy things. They made fun of me, as I ate that entire bowl of spaghetti. My sister Catherine, even as an adult, did not eat spaghetti and meatballs. It takes very little to innocently mold people to dislike, distrust, and sometimes hate what they don't know or understand.

"As I reconsider and think of our lives, I remember fun things like the spaghetti experience and also how often we were picked on because we were poor."

"Don, it feels to me that your people may not have had any money, but you had wealth. You actually were rich in love and affection. Money does not buy that. A lot of people feel if they have money they will be happy. I do not think that to be true."

"Evie, it was not easy. One day, after school my sister Irene fought two kids who made fun of her and her brown coat. They cornered her by the statue of the Holy Mother of God and tore one of her coat pockets. To them it was fun; I heard them laugh when I turned the corner to meet my sister. I cried. I was such a little guy. When we got home my mother sewed the pocket back, and no one could ever tell it had been torn.

"My mother could have a been a psychologist. While she was sewing, she told us how often people were bullies because they did not know who they were, and mostly because they were unhappy. They had to make others feel bad, or make fun of them if they were different. They felt this behavior made them bigger and better than they were. She also told us since the bad behavior did not make them feel better they had to keep on bullying people. I believe later on in my life, because of this incident, I learned to pay attention to the financial status of people. I made it a point to help those whose lives I could make better. Often in my real estate business, I gave some folks the money they needed for the down payment on houses they wanted to buy.

"I had a friend who believed I wanted sales so badly I gave people money to buy houses. The poor fellow had no idea what it was to have no money."

"Don, it is so wonderful to hear your stories. Your upbringing may have been moneyless, but I know you never lacked for the attention of your parents. "

"Ha, Evie, my mother was not an educated woman, but within what she learned in school, and maybe while observing around her, she developed common sense and gratitude. I can also say she was a woman with wisdom.

"Eveline, if there is one thing that is sad, it's that no one in my family ever talked about how they felt about being so poor. We were all accustomed not to speak a word about the conditions of our lives. So it all became normal. Irene told the stories of poverty but never how she felt about all of it. My sister Catherine never talked about being poor. We had rituals. On Sunday night, we ate navy bean soup, and that was normal. On Monday night we had a loaf made mostly of stale bread, and that, too, was normal. In other words, our conditioning was normal. I think hearing the stories from my sisters, I resolved early in life never to put wife or kid through such difficulties. Turns out, I gave them plenty of material things, and plenty of grief. Drinking like a fish, that too became normal."

"Don, I know in the United States there is no such thing as recognized castes. Or people do not talk about the differences in people's social classes. Yet, I suppose according to our station in life you and your family belonged to a lower group of people. Ultimately, we view the world with different eyes. You are a lucky man because with all that you described, you never once said you missed being loved because you had a lot of that. Your mother gave her family that strength. Lucky man! If I knew your mother, just about now, I would hug her."

"So, Evie, now you have an idea of what poverty looked like in my family. You are not entirely correct about the castes, but there is some resemblance to a caste system here. We just don't give it a name. One thing I am sure of, though we were poor, we had pride. I think rich or poor, this is something that may be missing in a lot of lives today."

"Wow! Don, to know you now, it is hard for me to conceive of such poverty. What is incredible is that because of some sort of bonding within the family, apparently none of you suffered the effects of your beginnings. I can only imagine the stress your parents experienced, and yet, they were able to render their children strong people despite the circumstances. I am at a loss for words. This is not something you see often anywhere."

"Evie, I believe there was a lot of love between us and somehow tolerance had to be part of it. Our entire place was smaller than our living room here. My mother used to bless even the people she did not really like. Now I say *Namaste* with the same intention.

"As for the poverty, let me tell you again, if you don't know you are poor, life is pretty normal. I guess most of our friends were equally poor, so we did not miss anything other kids had. We had enough to eat, we talked a lot, and that, my dear, as I told you before, is something I took from my beginnings. That and books! I was pleased the first time I came to your home to find bookcases everywhere. Happier to realize we read a lot of the same books."

"Gosh, I remember before we got married, sorting books out and deciding which one of us had a better looking copy of the same title. All along saying we will never buy another book. That was a promise neither of us could keep. It is a malady without cure."

"I have a feeling, books and yarns for your loom hold the same importance."

A Table for Two

"You know, Evie, I am glad books and conversations are an integral part of our lives. I like that about us. I know a hundred times I told you. Today is a good day to remind you again."

As he talked I looked at the multitude of books we had accumulated.

"Ha, Mr. Dailey, I am being formal here. I use the snobbery necessary for a particularly strong cup of coffee and the impertinence to serve it on a well decorated table. Those are rituals that are important to me. I grew up with cloth and silver. I can tell you, any food you serve with elegance tastes better."

He was no longer surprised when he saw my table settings. I believed, since the crooked smile or the raised eyebrows were not present, I knew he had gotten accustomed to my arrangements.

"Don, my children tell me my coffee has medicinal value. Do you think they are right?"

"Evie your coffee is very strong. Your kids are right."

"While I am at it, I am sorry for not giving you cereal. I could not conceive of eating the dried tasteless things coming out of a box. The corn or the wheat implied on the box, no one could ever recognize."

"Evie, I do not need anything special, I am happy with what you prepare for me. By now I know, the purpose of beautiful settings on a table is to make conversations flow with delight. Your manners and polish come through very well. You create the ambiance for storytelling. I like that.

"Evie, I like that we can discuss from politics, religion, human behavior, including your own, not forgetting the mundane nonsense of life. This is the stuff that rounds our lives. What many people don't know is that once one learns to separate passion and emotions, all conversations are possible, and constructive, because they are coming from the head and knowledge. I guess you would say, the art of diplomacy of your family must have ingrained some good senses into that thick head of yours."

"Yes, Don I must say, I am often affronted because I encounter a multitude of people without the very sense you are talking about. People born of foreign soil naturalized or not do notice that about the people of the USA. While Americans think the people making such observations and talking about them should go back wherever they came from they fail to realize they could acquire some polish and knowledge of other cultures. Those are loaded subjects most people are afraid or unable to look at."

"Evie, did you come here to have a better life?"

"Goodness no! I came here after conning my mother. My idea was I would meet Elvis Presley. I knew once he met me he would fall in love and we would live happily ever after. I was just sixteen then. What an ordeal that would have been!

"I suppose most people come here because they think they are going to find money on the ground. Well, my first dream did not manifest. Instead, I went to school. I learned English. My teachers from Germany and Great Britain were on task, and determined to teach me. They were great, but I hated them. Don, the first days in school were difficult. I did not understand a thing. Being homeschooled I had never been with so many people. They were rude, all of them.

"At the time, I wanted to be a researcher. I had many things in mind. I was young. Archeology and physics were my passions, after Elvis of course. Being somewhat of an artist, I also dreamed of painting my way into museums. I did not study archeology. Physics gave me a subtle understanding and an appetite for all things cosmic. I wanted to know about the order of numbers and geometry to grasp what was keeping the universe in check. Ultimately, art won. I had a few good art shows while in school. I received some ribbons and even sold a piece of art to a person with lots of money. The small painting you often admire comes from that era. My love of texture and colors probably came from my mother's ancestors and studying design became the easy thing to do. I cannot say my life has been easy in the USA, but it has been and continues to be a rich life.

"By now you know I live life without fear.

"Don, if this beautiful table could talk, it would speak of a distinguished gentleman."

As I said that, he looked at me, moved the corner of the tablecloth, examined the polished wood. The table was over one hundred years old. Satisfied that the wood grain had not changed he took my hand with his left hand. I had come to understand that this was the hand connected to his heart.

"Don, it is a pleasure to sit across from you. A man I know who found ways to educate himself. Because of your circumstances you learned to care genuinely about your fellow men and your wife too. This is a good table for great discussions. As I said before, you are a remarkable and magnanimous man. The table would say that too. I would come up with better adjectives, but each time I think of your qualities the same two words show up on my mind. It must be that language thing. You are stuck with the words I know."

"Evie, sometimes you amuse me. After so many years, I have not yet figured out if you are entertaining you or me more? As for linguistics, others may be confused by your accent, but I know how well you command the language and your mind. Why you describe me as you do confuses me. I am just a man.

"I have studied the behavior and psychology of people. You describe me as a magnanimous man. That, sweetheart, I am not. I am generous when I feel that I can be. That does not make me special in any way. Anyone with the means can do as I have done if they want to. Ultimately, I have come to believe that a systematic flow of rhythm and light is responsible for all you think I am. I express my life to suit my needs. That is selfish, not magnanimous, but I prefer to think that I live my life to serve my own truth."

"Don, if I must be honest, I believe we both lived our lives to serve our own truth and needs. We happen to choose to help others when we can. I guess it is the stuff we are made of. I stick to my words! I think your upbringing may have put a hindrance in your ability to look at yourself and say, *I am great*! I bet some priest or one of your nuns would find a sin there.

"We will have to continue the praises later on. I must answer the phone. It is your kidney doctor. I love this woman. How many doctors ever call their patients?"

Whenever I spoke to the various doctors treating my husband, I took notes, a different kind of notes. My dear husband must have skipped anatomy classes, I was sure of it. To him each organ operated separately. After all, he had a different doctor for each ailing part. He had a hard time accepting that his leaky heart affected his congested lungs or that his one kidney was busy cleaning his blood, something two kidneys do for most people. On the phone, he heard me say fantastic and he was pleased. That was enough for him.

This young woman, who studied about the nephritic system, was a holistic doctor. She understood the connection between all organs in relation to the person she was treating. Her specialty was the kidneys. She reported, after the latest blood tests, kidney, heart and lungs were functioning to the best of their capacities. All numbers were fine. She asked me how we were doing and reminded me to use her personal phone number if we needed to.

My conversation with this great gal prompted more talking. I told Don I wanted his cardiac doctor released from services. Two days before, during Don's monthly appointment, this man, standing by his office door without entering the room, told Don and me without an ounce of compassion that he had six months to live. I was furious, not because of the pronouncement we already knew, but because of a lack of humanity, a lack of diplomacy, a lack of savoir-faire. This man must have felt he was some sort of a god, but to me a swine was better.

We had read about all the maladies escorting death, we knew the prognosis for each.

That day, the hazel of Don's eyes became nearly purple. We gazed at each other, holding each other's hands. It was time for a passionate kiss. Moments later, we left the room. In the car we were speechless a while. Within a mile traveled he decided we needed to stop at the supermarket. Time for ice cream was upon us. At home, around the old table, an enormous bowl of ice cream brought delight to this man. His eyes regained their colors.

In complete denial of the elephant in the room, we chose to exercise the best pleasures of the flesh.

Six months came and went. Silently, we both had been counting days.

"Don, I am going to make you a great breakfast. What would you like?"

"Eggs, bacon, toast with lots of butter and jam, coffee and juice. I think that's a breakfast for the champion I am. Evie, before you say anything, remember, I may have a thousand things wrong with me, but cholesterol is not a problem. Today we celebrate because I am alive! This day we are celebrating the passage of time."

We laughed. I recognized the vibrations of lungs not filled to capacity. The cough instead of exhalation suggested a sound like a tin can rolling down a pebbled alley. I knew the implication of this simple laughter. The breakfast had to wait. It was time instead for a breathing treatment. While he took in oxygen, I hurried to the grocery store.

My husband had his breakfast. He was in bed where he had lusted after Canadian bacon. Once more, something had changed.

We had just left the six-month mark behind.

"So Evie, six months are gone and I am still alive. The idea of having a diet with low salt, and not enough sugar is not what I want. I need celebrations all day, and every day.

"By the way, no need to tell the kids. Their lives are difficult enough. They do not need to worry about me. Besides, the six months have passed, they did not know about it either. Don't tell them.

"I hope you know how sorry I am, putting you through all this. We know based on my age I do not have much time. The six months the doctors talked about are now gone, but that doesn't mean anything changed. We both know that.

"Eveline, remember before we got married more than once I told you if things did not go the way you expected, we could end the marriage? The option is on the table and it is for you to decide."

I paused, took a long breath, but this time, a furious explosion came out from my entire being. I felt rage like I never did before. This was the first time in our marriage that I believe I lost my mind. My voice told me so. I spoke to him in French. I was angry with all that I knew, including myself. I attempted to escape any way I could, but alas, nothing worked. It was during this momentary insanity, I remembered that I decided I was going to do all I could to keep this man alive. One more day, and another day, and another one after that, I screamed at him! I cried. I screamed! I was desperate. I cried some more.

"Come here, crazy wife. We both need a hug."

For a long time, we remained quiet. My dying husband protected me from emotions of love and despair I did not know I had and could not control. His chest wet with my tears did not bother him. As he did most nights, he ran his fingers through my hair, caressing my head until I fell asleep.

"Don, I do not want you to die. Your doctors are a bunch of quacks!"

"Evie, what do you want any doctor to do? Sweetheart, we know this is a part of my journey. We each have one, this journey is mine, and you can't go with me."

"I want to talk to your kidney doctor again. There is a body here, a whole body! You are not your maladies. You said so yourself. So I want to talk to her about you."

He took my hands, kissed them with a softness I blessed and cursed. He told me he agreed with what I was screaming about, and he reminded me he could hear me. He told me he understood my anger.

"You know Dailey, you piss me off!"

He hugged me again.

We visited the kidney doctor once more. She simply looked at us from the edge of the table in her office. She moved toward a great painting of various organs. She pointed to heart, lungs, and one kidney.

"Mr. Dailey these organs are part of your trio, they work together. You have no pain so I am going to do what I can to keep it that way. I need your good attitude to trust in your body. I will do all I can to handle the rest."

He coughed, not as a response, but something that came when he needed oxygen. She had not heard it before. She opened a drawer and out came the scope. This tall woman, now bending way down, started going up and down his chest with her stethoscope. She needed to listen to the pair of malfunctioning lungs. She ordered some more x-rays and a visit to a buddy of hers. She diagnosed nothing, but gave us a prescription for another inhaler. She pulled her chair, very close to us this time. She took one hand from each of us and held them. She wanted to know how we were doing emotionally. We spoke at length. Eventually, it was time to leave the office. She gave each of us a hug and said:

"Mr. Dailey you live until there is no life left. You have work to do around here. I want to see you next week when the x-ray report comes back to me. Here is my cell number again, don't lose it, and call me any time!"

We left her office with prescriptions to pick up at our pharmacy. One to render the heart stable, one to slow it down, one to give it a kick-start when too slow, and of course, the new inhaler. The fired heart doctor had transferred the files to her. Looking at her computer, she ordered a heart monitor, a blood pressure machine, and one more oxygen-measuring gadget. She looked at us and told us she would also order a better delivery of oxygen in the house. She told us this would be a tank, and not bottles of oxygen. Those were used only when going out. I visualized our bedroom with one more item belonging in a hospital. She saw my face, and told me this tank would be in the garage, and I would have to cope with the plastic tubes throughout the house. I cried and laughed; she did these things, and they were all part of her non-diagnosis.

Before the parting, her instructions to him were: "No strenuous exercises since an aorta with a hole has a tendency to leak or tear completely. Your left ventricle is enlarged, but everything is where it needs to be." She even instructed us about sex. With heads full of a mixture of hope and acceptance for an eventual outcome, we agreed to give it all a try. After one more hug, she patted both of us and said, "You know Mr. Dailey, you are a walking miracle. Take care of her so she can take care of you."

While driving back home, Don and I once more talked about the value of life and how most people lived knowing about the death of people around them, but somehow lived as if this momentous event were applicable only to others.

In one afternoon my title changed from wife to the resident panic-stricken nurse.

Once settled at home, again we talked more about the value of life—our lives. At this point in our journey, knowing about death outside our door, consciousness became abundant.

Passion, emotions and fear flooded my mind and my heart. All that I could feel came crashing in; I could not stop this tornado. The man who controlled and steadied his life like a Swiss watch had to face unanticipated challenges. His wife had gone mad. Somehow, he found a method to comfort me while accepting what was going on with his body.

"Evie, all this news, pills and expectation of death are all challenging, but let's try to remember, we are alive only for however long we are supposed to be. So let's live. Since you and I have not escaped to the other side, wherever that is, we must still have things to learn and things to do. You better talk to me about what is going on inside. Again, if you can't handle it, I will understand."

"Don, I am angry because we all take our lives for granted. Now I am faced with the need to accept the things I cannot change. I do not like it one bit! I must find a way to induce gratitude in my heart for all that I have *now*. I know we both take better care of our cars than we do our bodies. I guess we both must change gears."

"Well, Evie I know this car will not go back to the dealer. Any repair must come from some other garage. You're angry because you can't control what's going on. I understand that fully. You know I had to learn about detachment when my first wife finally had enough of me. I think you are experiencing the same type of anger. Sweetheart, don't go there, you don't want to be robbed of precious energy. Besides all that, I like to see you smile and laugh. Now more than ever I need your laughter."

Consoling each other the best we could, he went on about his life as I did mine. The need to inform his or my children of events in our lives did not feel urgent. There was something freeing about this acceptance. Yet we knew we were robbing them of emotions they were entitled to. Once that was handled, all we had to do was live.

As the clock moved forward, the stories he told became shorter. The breath entering the lungs became labored. Reading instead of talking changed the focus. Life may have had its own plans, but we had laughter mixed with all sorts of oddities.

One morning he came to the table with his yellow pad and a coin: a silver dollar. He sat, and placed the coin in front of me. As often before I was totally confused.

"Well, Don if you are going to give me a coin why not go for the gold? Since you know I am not much into collecting silver dollars, you better tell me about this coin. And does it have a meaning I need to know?"

"Evie, of course it has meaning. Everything has meaning. I came to a conclusion about this coin. I was thinking, we all forget that a coin has two sides. The life of humanity is all about denial and delusions because we look at everything around us with one idea. We walk around with blinders. Let's talk about the hidden side of this coin, the hidden side of life—the side that comes with pain and shame that we all carry. We better explore this coin from all sides and learn that one does not own a coin without owning both surfaces. We all seem to concern ourselves mostly with the head on the coin. We do the same with our body. We concern ourselves only with a part of ourselves and hide the rest. I think all the diseases I have acquired are like the back of that coin. I now must look at all sides and that means facing all the issues attached to my life and its end. I don't like it. I would prefer to live a lot longer, but I know I am not getting better because I feel it. I don't know when I will die, I must order some more coins. I want each of my grandchildren to have one."

"That's it? And what am I to do with the coins and the grandchildren? They will miss or not miss you, and that will be their individual choice and feeling. They will think of you only according to their individual development in life."

"Eveline, let me explain. One day, after I am dead, you will know when to do it. I suggest you give a coin to each of my grandchildren. I can't leave them fortunes, but I think the coin will provide them with this idea that I have. You know if I had given any thought to my fortune, I could have left them each a house. Who knew I would not be able to? I don't know about other people, but I know I did not think about things like that."

"You better tell me about this idea because you lost me when you put the coin on the table. You really know how to confuse me."

"My idea is that my grandchildren need to know the coin. It represents life, Evie. They need to familiarize themselves intimately with both sides. The coin is only a metaphor. If they are lucky, they will understand the symbol. The coin represented their bodies, their lives, and all that they are. It is also work and play. Everything around us has more than one side. I hope they can realize that life itself is two-sided. They can choose to live the illusions of a one-sided life. They can choose a life with one vision, and one idea. They can also choose a real life that is offered with all its subtleties. They can live life for its façade, or they can turn the coin and see what their lives stand for. In other words, they need to know the worth of their lives. This is not about money. This is about value."

During our tête-à-têtes, stories hidden in the shadows of time found their way to bright light. He did not know he was a teacher. He walked a path where few had ever stepped. I know, Don, the man I married, was an example few could ever follow.

"Evie, you speculate too much. I thought you were taking notes about my life? How about we continue? Are you up to the task today? I am remembering about school. How about telling you about that? Get the pad and the pen."

First Impressions of School

"Since you seem to be asking me about every bit of my life, I will tell you about my first go around with school. I know being mostly home-schooled; you escaped what many other children experience. I don't know if that's good or bad.

"As you would say; it started on a wonderful day in September in 1935.

"It was cool in upstate New York. The leaves of the maple trees on both sides of our street were yellow and orange with a lot of brown. Almost nothing green was left. I was six years old. Would you believe I remember this as if it were yesterday? My mother told me only special boys went to Sacred Heart School in Utica, New York.

"My two older sisters were in the same school. By the way, they were my first teachers. Because of them, I knew how to write and I could read a lot. The teachers in that school were all nuns. My very first class was to learn to draw and Sister—I don't remember her name— was roaming the room without ever stopping. We were drawing an apple because of Eve from the Bible. She was a sinner. Now I wonder why this was the first drawing class. I did not understand what the nun was saying, but it did not matter. I was drawing.

"At the time the nuns wore their habits. She had a white coif on. I am telling you, if she had a broom she could have flown right out of the room. Her black habit and the white scapular made her look like a sick penguin. That apron so starched it looked like wood. She also had a rosary hanging from a belt. She must have had special shoes on because I didn't hear her coming up behind me. She gave my left hand a really hard swat with a pointer she always carried. The top of my left hand bled. I dropped my pencil and the point broke. She hit me again. I wanted to cry or run away, but I didn't. For a long time I was convinced she was a witch. Now I know people of weak character seem to have a need to bully others. She was a bully for sure.

"All she did that day was shout at me. 'In Catholic schools there will be no left-handed writing.' She went on with this for the entire hour. In the meantime, my hand was hurting. It was red and there was blood too. It was the first time I realized that I held my pencil with the 'wrong' hand. The devil's hand she even said. I don't know where she got this idea. My daddy wrote with his left hand and my mother and sisters used their right hands, but nothing was ever said about the left hand. I knew that if it were wrong, my daddy would not be doing it. For sure Sister was an evil witch."

"Don, I guess you need to know what I feel about the priesthood and sisterhood or whatever they are called. They are all in it for the power they have over others. That woman must have been one frustrated person! I bet you some family member probably decided she would become a nun. Who knows? Maybe she wanted to be a stripper."

"Evie, you are funny. At this time in my life, I didn't know a sister was a woman. All I knew, they were special people doing God's work. I never understood it because she was so mean. This is what I was told, and my mother didn't lie. She returned next to my desk, and for the hundredth time she screamed, all of God's children were to write with the right hand. She also said, if she ever caught me using my left hand for writing she would hit me ten times. In the course of my first year I was wacked many times. It took a long time but I did learn to write with my right hand. I got wacked because the letters I wrote did not look good, and generally, she did not like me."

"Don, do you think such behavior continues today in Catholic schools? I feel the emotional and physical damage done to children in the name of God is pathetic.

"Eveline, I know it's not only the fate of children. We continue to damage and kill people in the name of God. That will not change in my lifetime. It truly makes no difference what religion people are. Soldiers kill because they are told to, and their religions tell them not to kill but they must listen to the generals. I believe religions are in place to control people. Generals are not far behind. Based on my observation, I think they are all doing well with their need to control."

"You have a point, Evie! I remember going home after that first day and telling my mother how my left hand was hurting and I showed her the cut part and the hand was still red and swollen. My mother, being the first generation Irish Catholic would not confront the church, the nuns or the priests. In school I was to obey the sisters: they knew best. I asked about daddy writing with his left hand and my mother said, 'Daddy did not go to a Catholic school.' You have a very good point about control, Evie. When my daddy came home, I tried to get support from him; he told me it was probably better to be right-handed, because most people were. He offered no explanation for what he said.

"My parents were prisoners of a system they never questioned or understood. I still remember some books I read about WWII. Everyone wore blinders. When it comes to control that's the way it works.

"I hated every moment I was at school. I was the smallest kid and everyone made fun of me. My shoes had holes at the bottom that my father fixed with cardboard and when some kids saw that, they really bullied me around. When I told my mother, she told me they were bad kids. She could not bring herself to go to the school and talk to Sister. I think that left-hand and right-hand thing left some deep scars in more than my hands."

This was something that had happened eighty years before and yet I could see the pain of the boy in his face. Growing up with pride yet in abject poverty and no emotional support from home or school must have been a challenge that left deep scars indeed. Somehow, with work and difficulty he overcame the turmoil of his youth. When he told me as a young adult he drank in excess, I could not help but wonder if the early life's ordeals could have been one of the causes. When I asked him about this, he only said, "in life we all have choices to make." He was correct.

"The second year was better. I had a new sister as my teacher. The old witch was too old and could not teach anymore. I was now right-handed, but not 100 percent. I still did some things as a left-handed person, and in my heart I knew that God did not care one way or another. I was young and there were many things I did not understand about God. Well, come to think of it, I still don't know.

"Evie, I was surprised when you remarked every time I lost something like my keys, wallet or glasses; you told me it never failed, you found whatever it was on the left side of where I had been last. You are observant. It's obvious my brain kept its dominant side."

We talked about the disservice the nuns did to him and all the kids that were left- handed. I suppose at the time they did not know about the hemispheres of the brain and dominant sides or synapses and so on. Unlike many left-handed people in history, he was not artistic, but again, he was never given the opportunity to try his hands at any art. If he had an artistic side he never had time to explore it.

That was the way for the poor.

"You know, Evie, something else I discovered because of something you said: we were poor, but our clothes were always clean and pressed and my mother could mend anything a hundred times. When today, I see children in dirty clothes; I can almost see my mother washing our clothes by hand. Today people have washing machines and too often I see kids with dirty clothes. The times have changed a lot.

"Perhaps the parents of today are not told to keep their children clean. I see a lack of pride in people. They are not proud of themselves, so they can't bring that to the lives of their children."

"The only good thing about this school was the librarian, Father Julian.

He was an old priest. He let me stay and read in the small room that was called a library. Our bookshelves contain more books than the school library did, but it was the largest one I had ever seen. It had a long table and many chairs. I could stay there and read for hours. Sometimes when I did not understand a word, I would ask Father and he spent time explaining it to me. He was a good man, Irish also. He told me he came from the same county as my mother. He had to be a good person."

A First Communion

"Evie, I am telling one story after the other, but you have not told me the story about going into the *Inepe*. You know, I can't wait forever, I don't have forever!"

"Don, I will make a deal with you. After you give me the communion details I will tell you. After you eat something!"

"So now you know about my early life in and out of school. Let's see what damage I can do with the first and foremost important sacrament in the life of an Irish Catholic boy. I already told you when I was a baby my mother dedicated me to the Church. That meant I was to become a priest. The first communion was something important to my mother. I, on the other hand, was interested in the presents I would get."

"Donaldo! How could your mother decide what you would become as an adult? Never mind, my mother decided who my first husband would be. I guess it is the same. Parents think they can control the lives of their children. They did not know to rear their children instilling the concepts of personal choice. Our lives proved that to impose parental will is not always possible."

"So, let me tell you what I remember about this most significant event. I think that and the priesthood my mother had planned would have crowned her accomplishments. Alas, and gladly so, it did not happen.

"It was on a Sunday morning in early May in 1935. At the store where they sold and sometimes gave clothes away, my mother found me the perfect suit. It did not need a lot of altering. Of course, she washed it and it turned out to be the whitest thing I had ever seen. Dressed up, in white, my mother said I was clean and pure to receive Holy Communion. I felt like an angel, but I had no wings. Sacred Heart Parish church was a two-mile walk from our place, but that was fine. It was an important day and the weather was great. Everyone in the family was all dressed up, my father wearing his only suit. He got it many years before from the same place my suit came from. Come to think of it, all our clothes came from the basement of the church. My mother could fix anything. She made our clothes look great and new. She was also in her best outfit and my sisters were wearing their Sunday clothes. Sacred Heart Church and the school were in a three-story building. I think the only church and school like that in Utica. All the kids dressed in white were in second grade. That's when good Catholics receive their first communion. All the girls with white dresses and the boys all dressed like me looked really good and pure. Many times, as we walked toward the church, my mother reminded me not to kick any rocks because it was an extra special day for my soul. I never understood what the rocks and my soul had in common. I did not kick any rocks and my shoes stayed clean.

"You know what, Evie, since you always say you want to come back as a rock, maybe she knew something about that? Kicking rocks, I could have been hurting your relatives."

"Don, I am coming back as a boulder, not some small pebble."

"It was a long mass, with singing and incense, and I was hungry. You know to receive communion you must fast. After the Mass everyone went in front of the church to give hugs. In my six-year-old observation, I was sure half the world was there. I just wanted to get home; my folks were having a party for me. The guests would arrive at 2:30 in the afternoon. Before they came I would be given something to eat.

"When we finally got home, off went my white clothes and the shoes until about fifteen minutes before the guests arrived. I was to stay pure and clean all day; I think this was the hardest part. I ate some oatmeal. I had energy, but couldn't do anything. I can't say I was having fun.

"I needed money so I kept imagining how much I would get.

"I knew all the people who would be there, cousins and two of my mother's friends. There were some cousins of mine that I did not like, but I was not supposed to say that.

"Before I could get comfortable doing nothing, I heard my mother, 'Hurry up, Donnie. Finish dressing and keep them clothes white! Wait a minute! Is that a black mark on your white shoe, how did that happen? I looked down and it was true. My left shoe had a black mark on it. 'Mom, I don't know how that happened I'll try to get it out.' People were coming in and I was saved."

Saved by Family and Friends

Thank God, some family arrived and I did not have to go clean my shoe right then. I would have to after the company was gone. Dad left the room and my mother followed. The guests had to go to the backyard where there was a long table ready to receive the food people would bring. Chairs were scattered everywhere. Everything came from neighbors and the church. We only had five chairs and our table was not that big. I still slept under it and since I was growing, my feet passed the end of my fort.

"There were a lot of people filling up the house and the yard. My mother's friends were the worst ladies I ever met. They gave me hugs, almost choking me, telling me that I looked like an angel. I kept thinking, how long did I have to put up with this before I start opening my gifts and counting my money? I wondered also if the food came before or after the gifts. People were just talking too much. My Dad told me not to expect much money because there was a great depression in America. People had very little money. My dad used himself as an example. He told me he worked for $3.00 a week, and he was happy to have that job because many men had no job at all.

"None of my friends from school were at my party because they were having their own. You have no idea; our family was endless; I recognized them all except one man talking to my Dad. I was called over and he introduced me to Mr. Morgan, who was the owner of the house we were living in. He was from another state and worked in the factory where Ford cars were made. He must have been someone important, or maybe I was that important. I am sure my daddy would tell me about him later.

"Right after meeting Mr. Morgan, I found out we were going to eat first, before the cards and gifts. Though I eat slowly, that day I swallowed my food so fast I don't think I chewed anything. I was in a hurry to count my money. Finally, the cards and gifts were ready to be opened. I got some books because everybody knew I liked to read. I had to open every card and read it so people would applaud. So silly, but I kept on reading. In 1935 this second grader could read very well, and I liked to read, but some of the handwritings were not easy to decipher. It looked like I received a lot of dimes and few quarters and two one-dollar bills. The last card was still in my hand when my Dad's friend Mr. Morgan called me. 'Hey Donnie I really did not know this was your First Communion day so I have no card, but here's your gift. A brand-new-looking $5.00 bill just for you.'

"He told me that it was President Lincoln's picture. Lots of people clapped and Mr. Morgan placed the $5.00 bill into my shirt pocket. Right away my Dad called me and reminded me to say thank you, but I already had thanked Mr. Morgan, my hero of the day. My dad asked me to let him keep the money safe for me. I begged him to let me keep my money. It was my first $5.00 bill ever! I had never seen one before.

'Don't lose it' my father said, and with that off I went with my $5.00 in my shirt pocket.

There Was a Thief

"People finally left. I wanted to know exactly how much money I had, but first I had to change clothes and help my mother and father with cleaning up. The chairs and tables were returned where they belonged—our chairs back to the house. When I was done, Dad, who was on the porch, called me over, 'Well Donnie you've done okay with the money. You have four books, you are lucky, one book is a new. You have $4.75 plus the $5.00 from Mr. Morgan. Let me have it so we can keep it safe in a secured place.'

"Evie, telling you this story over eighty years later, I can still feel the pain in the pit of my stomach. I went to get the money out of my pockets. When my hand reached into the shirt pocket, nothing was in it. Tom Dailey was a 100 percent Irishman. He did not drink, but he had a temper, and it exploded that Sunday afternoon of my communion.

"With the help of my sisters along with my mother, Dad and I looked for the money until dark. The $5.00 bill was missing. It had vanished. $5.00 was more than a week's pay for my Dad. I was 98 percent sure I knew who left my party with my new President Lincoln bill. I could not say anything bad about the person. We did not say bad things about family or anyone else. I kept my mouth shut.

"I felt it when he pulled the money out of my pocket. I think I was too stunned; it was a relative.

"My First Communion ended with me having a different view of life. People were not very honest, not all of them, anyway, not when money was involved. I also learned and accepted that I was responsible for my loss. One of my cousins was not an honest person. My mother, good as always, said that the person who took the money must have needed it more than we did. I know that cousin did not need my money, but I could not name him; that would not have been acceptable. I went in my fort, and I cleaned my white tarnished shoes."

"Don, this must have been a traumatic experience for you. Coming from a world where to be able to say who took your money was wrong would have sent me over the edge."

"Evie, life has a way of going on no matter what happens. Did I tell you, soon after my communion, during that second grade year, I was pulled out of school because I started stuttering badly? Today, I know after enough studies, not being able to talk about this event, and not being able to name the thief may have been responsible for a psychological break. What I knew to be wrong could not be spoken of. Clinically speaking, this was the cause of the stuttering. I have no doubt.

"As I got older, I realize that most of the people I end up assisting in recovery have been traumatized not by strangers, but mostly by relatives. The closer the relative, the greater the damage; this can be measured in many human relationships.

"Somehow, I worked it out. The thief was a cousin. I also learned, that how we worked things out makes a difference in our lives. Remembering not to be bitter was not so easy! I learned to forgive but that did not mean I ever forgot.

"Sometimes when I was unable to speak comprehensibly, the nuns would go to my sister Irene's class and have her come to my room and interpret what I was trying to say. It was pretty bad. Then I would get mad and stop talking altogether. There is a black American poet who was raped by a relative when she was very young. She too stopped talking for a very long time. Like me, because of the family relationships she too could not name the person. Have you ever heard of Maya Angelou? I have one of her books. I think you would enjoy it.

"Eventually with the help of my mother and her patience, I stopped stuttering, and returned to school. I don't know how she divined what to do, but she did a good job. Now you know why after that I never stopped talking."

"Wow, Don, you keep telling me stories of human behavior, and how what is done to or for people affects their lives. I am glad you talk a lot. How else would I know these things?"

I heard the details of the first communion, and I came to understand, that the incident taught him how to be humble, forgiving, but retaining the memory. He talked a while longer. My mind took me to another story he told me. This one was about a good friend who needed a large sum of money. Don had this large amount of money and lent it to his friend. Soon after the man became a millionaire. Don asked him to repay the debt, and the man had no recall of such a loan.

Rather than using the arm of the law to recoup his money, Don tore the promissory note. The man, at this time held a place of prominence. When I questioned his sanity, with regard to his friend, Don said:

"Evie, I believe, if we know our highest ideals, we all must serve them. I chose to serve mine because I could help a man in need. I was only being true to myself, and the principles that I live by. He, on the other hand, chose to serve his—greed."

As often I did, I remained speechless. He continued to talk.

"While I was in the 4th grade, we moved from the only house we had lived in since my birth. We were forced to move because my Dad always treated every rental like it was his house. He enjoyed planting, so for the seven or eight years we lived there he made the yard look like a park. The Owner, Mr. Morgan said his taxes were going to be increased, so he raised the rent. My folks could not afford the new rent. Mr. Morgan's greed taught me a good lesson. He gave when people were there to see what he was doing, and applaud him. When no one was there watching, his greed took over.

Many Lessons

"Evie, every event, every thing that ever happened in my early life had a lesson for me to use later on in life.

"When I began to buy houses and rent them, if a tenant did any improvements I would not raise their rent. I may have held the papers, but it was their home. I purchased low to mid-income rentals. The people who lived in my homes were not rich. Sometimes they even needed a little help."

"I have seen you lowering rent for people who were having a hard time. Don, I don't think I ever met another human being who would do this. In my book you are remarkable, and I call you a patriarch because I think a patriarch would take care of his flock as you did. I know your heart, Don Dailey. It is not your pocket that dictates your actions. Yes, a remarkable patriarch, that's what you are!"

"Evie, this only means that I was free to pursue the things I was able to. I am lucky today, and was then as well. I was able to follow my bliss as Joseph Campbell eloquently explained in his books.

"My going to a monastery was part of my spiritual development. Incorporating the Religion Sciences from Ernest Homes to my life was an integral part of my growth just as the monastery was. This, by the way, was part of the philosophies, spiritual and metaphysical of the New Thought movement of which I am still a practitioner. You saw the papers when I was the officiating minister at some of my grandchildren's marriages. You have heard me talk at their churches. I learned a great deal from each group. Evie, there were many teachers around to influence my growth. Joel Goldsmith added important, and significant ideologies to my life. From him it became clear that while I was looking for fulfillments outside of myself, it was all an inside job. Lao Tzu had made this abundantly clear, but he was from a different philosophy and culture. Sometimes I didn't digest all he said. Becoming a practitioner of many philosophies gave value to who I was becoming every day. I taught the Silva Mind Control method. Jose Silva was a great man and a good friend. His daughter continued the teachings. She renamed it, the Silva Method. I feel it's a better name. I was able to pursue all things because I had a desire to respond to my needs. I don't think too many people are aware of my spiritual pursuits. I don't think my children know much.

"Evie, I am sorry you never met Vetura Papki. She was the teacher, the mentor and the friend who influenced me the most. She brought the teachings of Religions Science and its practices to the best of my heart and soul. I met Louise Hay a couple of times. We were all from the same school. Vetura took me to where I needed to find that place within. She was a good friend. My healing practices mostly came from Religious Science principles. All of it is important in my life. All my teachers taught me to open myself to receive what God had to offer me. By the way, I am only a conduit while doing a healing treatment. Like you, Vetura and Louise were focused women. I think given the opportunity, if you chose you would be a good healer. You already do a lot of that. I don't know if these women counted all day long as you do, but I know they are women of measure.

"Evie, I don't know the words to tell you how much I appreciate you in my life. I am happy, and I enjoy telling you about my adventures, and the misadventures too. There is something that you extract from within me and it feels good."

"Don, you must tell me what that is."

"Sweetheart, you have taught me acceptance. I see that you have your opinions, strong ones too, but you don't attempt to tell others what they need to do. You express your opinions and after being around you, I realize they come from a good place. That, my dear, is a quality few have. You exercise acceptance without direction from your emotions. I notice you don't always practice this with your kids. I think I know why you are like that."

"Perhaps, mea culpa is in order. I suppose my children are my ego extension, and it is alive and well. I want my children to be perfect—by my standards of perfection, you understand."

"Evie, as you grew up, I am almost certain, you were told you were perfect. You wish the same for your children. I noticed often, your conversations with them are robust and to the point, based on who you are, they can only be that. As for the rest of the world, you do not get yourself emotionally attached. That's why your brother calls you a singular person."

"Well, Don, I have been hurt by many people. It is a matter of self-protection. I prefer not to have people trampling me. I am polite, but I keep most people away at an arm's length. By the way, that gives me more time to do what I want and not concern myself with how people feel. I am not the angel you think I am."

"Evie, I never thought you were an angel. I do know what they are supposed to be like. I don't think *you* are one."

We both laughed and he continued his elaboration about his family.

"Life was progressively more difficult for my parents. They didn't have money for basic necessities. We had to move into a Public Housing Project. We felt fortunate because the building was new, and it was the pride of the City of Utica. My mother told me all our neighbors were nice. I didn't have time to meet any. I worked long hours before and after school. We stayed in that place for about a year, I think.

"Did I tell you about the Irish girl? Evie, this is funny. She was about seventeen, and was married to a widower with two children. She was our next-door neighbor. She was pregnant when we moved to the project. She did not speak English well. She was learning. She once knocked on our door to ask my mother about a watermelon she purchased. She boiled it for dinner. Poor thing wanted to know what spices to put in the soup because it did not taste good and had completely fallen apart. I was in the kitchen when I heard her. I could not help it, but I burst out laughing. Later on, after she left, I got in trouble for not controlling my humor. My mother gave me a lesson about accepting the people that knew less than I did. That day, I learned not to laugh at people. I can tell you it was interesting living there! I also had to change school. This time I went to a public school and that was a very different experience.

"Fifth grade was the first time in my life without the Catholic nuns as my teachers. I was glad to find some left-handed kids in that school. By this time, however, I was able to write with my right hand. Most of the students were just kids like me, but they were not polite. You know, Evie, most parents did not seem to teach their children basic polite behavior. There were some black kids, more Italians, and of course, more Irish kids too—it was a very large school. I became friends with an Italian boy named Gino. I loved going to his house. I got to eat great foods. Overall the kids in that school had no manners. Some even talked back to the teachers.

"Evie, now I know why people send their children to Catholic school. They let the school handle the raising of their kids. Parents don't take the time to be engaged in the lives of their children. They let the school raise them. I was guilty of that with my boys. I sent them to Catholic school so I did not have to worry about them. I am not sure things are any different today. I am also guilty of putting my two girls in a different category. They became the responsibility of their mother.

"In my case, my parents did not like the public school system for me. The next year, I had to go back to Catholic school. For that, I had to walk or take the bus—when I could afford to. In my first class the nun was another witch. I knew to keep my mouth shut. I couldn't say anything about how bad she was—not only to me, but also to many other kids. I came from a home were my mother and father would not question the actions of a nun, or a doctor, or anyone they believed had authority. My parents had been conditioned to accept everything and question nothing.

"You know Evie, when I was young I didn't understand about cultural differences. My Italian or black friends were all people to have fun with."

The Sweat Lodge, or The *Inepe*

"Evie, you may not realize it, but you are different than other people I know. I have no doubt it all comes from the way you were brought up. There are times when you talk that you sound uncaring, yet I know you to be soft of heart and very generous. You call me a *patriarch* because I take care of an imaginary tribe. You are very much like me. Like me you started out by finding your own light. That, my dear, is enormous! You also do things other women wouldn't dare. What woman do you know who allows people to reside in her home just because she likes art and artists?

"I also can't think of any woman or man I know who would go into a Sweat Lodge. I still would like you to tell me more about that."

"Don, you have a point. I grew up with art and artists around me. I may have been influenced by my early surroundings to become a free thinker. I am not afraid of people, and for sure, having the ability to assist artists was an honor. I had the room to house them. And remember, there was a valuable exchange. I got to experience the birth of magnificent music. I learned about sacred geometry. I saw the development of great art. Everyone took part in and gained from this exchange. I had help to care for the property, they had the right setting to expand their gifts."

"Evie, I know you do what rings true to you. Your understanding of freedom does not attach you to political or religious endeavors. You accept that you are a spiritual being. Good for you!

"The other day you told me you did not particularly like children, yet at Gardens for Humanity you worked with hundreds of them. Here I am jumping subjects again. Forget that, and tell me about this *Inepe* thing. Any woman I know would not be around a fire pit with people she does not know—unless alcohol and loud music was involved. You do not have a sense of fear. I want to explore this with you. First, tell me about your experience in the sweat lodge."

"Alright Don, to explain this to you, I must first take you to where it all began. You are correct. I do not entertain the idea of fear as a pastime.

"I can say, it was by accident that I ended up inside an *Inepe*. Living as I do, I know, the universe has a way of providing me with wonderful accidents, and plenty of protection.

"Because I live in the *now*, opportunities presented themselves magically. Each time I had a choice to make. It all started with an intriguing little store named Alpha Centauri. It begged for my exploration. It was not too far from where I lived. I made one stop, and my life began on a new journey.

"It took both hands to open this solid artful wood door. It was a work of art in its own right. Once inside, I noticed how small the place was. It was not well lit, and it was filled with treasures. Indigenous artifacts were on shelves. The most interesting handmade jewels were in glass cases. Pottery with handles made from deer antlers were also on shelves. The owner turned on additional lights. I could see details the various craftsmen had applied to their wares. Astonished by all I saw, I asked the owner about a piece of pottery. He was explaining a process to me when another person came in. They obviously knew one another. The large man was an American Indian. He introduced himself and told me he was from the Pima reservation. In the same breath, he asked: 'are you sweating with us tonight?' I was lost. I never before had met an American Indigenous person. I also did not understand what the question meant.

"Realizing that I did not understand, the two men proceeded with explanations. This was a special night, they said. I knew it was December and the temperature was going to drop. They told me about *Grandmother* being full. I asked who she was. They laughed, and told me indigenous people called the moon *Grandmother*. I was utterly confused. They again asked me if I was coming to the lodge. I asked what a sweat lodge was.

"The man said he had to go tend to the fire. He had a truck full of wood. Christopher, the owner of the store, realizing I did not understand offered me an explanation. The sweat lodge was on his property, and was made of curved willow branches. Sixteen long branches, not twigs, were placed in a way to form a dome. This low profile frame, after some horizontal solidification, was covered with layers of blankets. As he talked, he drew the shape of the structure so I could better visualize. At the center, he explained that there was a pit. It was about forty inches round and about a foot deep. Stones that had been in a raging fire all day were brought in, a few at a time. I still did not understand what he was talking about. He told me there were usually about a dozen people inside the *Inepe*. The idea of going in was to cleanse mind and soul, he explained.

"Don, he could have been speaking Chinese. Nothing made sense. I, however, listened.

"Christopher drew me a map because the lodge was on top of the mountain where his house was. He was the fire keeper, and the man I had met was the shaman. I felt I had stepped into the world of a Jules Verne of the Americas. Christopher also told me to wear cotton clothes and socks and to bring a towel. As I left his store, he shouted, bring a change of clothes. Part of the instruction included bringing some food to share.

"Driving the few miles home, I felt there must have been a reason why I met such people. Before entering my driveway, I decided I would go. Remember to wear only cotton clothes. Bring a towel. Bring some food to share with about twelve people. Not forgetting a change of clothes, all was mentally in place before I got out of my car."

"Evie, you are the one who is remarkable. Who in their right mind would ever consider doing something like that with people you didn't know?"

"Well Don, I never told you I was in my right mind. This whole thing simply felt right. I changed to the only white cotton knit pants and a top from Italy that I had. In December I did not wear cotton. I also wore socks. In the refrigerator, I had some cheese, crackers, ham and salami and other finger foods that I had purchased for a reception at the gallery the next day. I was set. I made a platter with some of the stuff, and put the tray on the passenger side of my car.

"The directions to get there were odd. I was not going to travel on the paved roads. There were no lights on the road. The piece of paper with drawing and markers was in my hand. It was excessively cold; I wore my down jacket.

"Following instructions, I drove, leaving the paved road. I made the first correct left turn, immediately after, a right one almost into a ditch. In front of me I saw the first marker: a small shed without a door. I took a slight left. Still driving at about two miles per hour, a few more feet, I saw the water tank. That was the second marker— an important one! I was not lost. A few more feet farther, there were some antennas from the local ham radio operator. This was a road for a mule. I kept wondering about the bottom of my car. I was certain the surface of the moon was smoother than where I was.

"Suddenly, before me, five parked cars. Intuitively, I knew—I had arrived. I stood a short while to give my eyes a chance to adjust to the moonlight. The temperature had dropped. I heard conversation and laughter coming from the top of the mountain. I followed the sound. My vision adjusted itself and I could see people. There was a raging fire burning and the people were standing around it. The fire-keeper noticed me. It was Christopher. He told me to go to the house, which was about two hundred feet from where I was. 'Put the food on the table, and come and join us.'

"Once inside the house, I fell in love with the interior. Indigenous art was displayed everywhere my eyes could see. While I wanted to see each piece individually, I turned to the front door, and went to join the others on the mountaintop. I did not know them. The narrow trail felt like climbing Mount Everest. I made it to the plateau. Everyone was waiting for me. They made me feel welcomed. My down jacket was greatly appreciated. One woman pointed for me to look to the left. I saw the *Inepe*. Like the drawing, it was a rounded structure covered with blankets. The entry was another blanket. The people around the fire were bent on explaining all I needed to know. I was, perhaps, being initiated. One told me the rocks were not ready— they were red hot. They needed to be blue.

"While waiting for heat to penetrate the last molecules of the rocks, lively discussions continued. At one point, the shaman entered the *Inepe*. People took off their coats. I did too. On a long bench, the coats formed a mountain. In front of this pile, shoes were left.

"I had to crawl to enter the odd structure. The shaman, who entered first, told each person where to sit. I was next to him. Soon, all the people were in, feet tucked close and not extended toward the empty pit. The fire keeper came in with a pitchfork-like tool and brought in stones the size of my head. Gently and with respect he placed stones in the center of the pit. He did this three times. The temperature inside became pleasant. At the second round of stones, I brought my feet very close to me. If I left them where they were they would end up cooked. In a clockwise order each person talked a bit. Between each round of talk, sets of stones were brought in. The formula was: four stones, one at a time, one for each of the four cardinal directions. The idea resonated with my own belief system. It got hotter inside. This process went on fourteen times.

"Don, you will never know how hot I felt, and still survived. In my honor the round of rocks brought into the *Inepe* stopped at fourteen. I did not ask about the numerical logic. The pile of red and blue hot rocks was high. I could barely see the people across from me. I was wet with perspiration from head to toes. Between each round the shaman threw some sweet herbs, sage, sweet grass and corn to the fire for purification. I think the sage took care of the smell of toxins we each must have released. I was ready to leave, but people kept talking. Sadness and happiness were discussed. I listened. I thought of my mother. She would have been horrified, not because I was with people I did not know, but because I was sweating. In my family, women did not sweat. There were no signs of the *Inepe* being vacated. I continued to think about my mother. I cried for her, and I smiled too. I felt gratitude. She had given me the gifts of self-sufficiency and also of self-assurance. She had prepared me to follow my own star.

"It was between my reveries that the shaman explained the number of the rocks brought in. Four stones at each round brought the number to fifty-six stones. Only two rocks should have been delivered during the last round. Making the number to fifty-two. The number of weeks in a year—I wanted to get out.

"I was also amazed that the smell of sweating people was non-existent. It was so hot I felt a layer of my skin could come off. Tears of pain ran down my face, and I could not tell if the tears were from physical or emotional pain. This was an experience about digesting who I was, and also what I was made of. I can also say it was a cleaning of the soul. If nothing else, I was releasing some toxins.

"A while later, between rounds, I realized I was not thinking at all. My mind was completely and utterly quiet. I am certain this did not happen as a result of something I could explain to myself, nor was it willed. My overactive mind had taken a holiday. Moments before, I could not imagine my body being so hot, and moments after I was looking toward a point of reference for and to myself.

"An eternity later, the shaman asked the fire keeper to open the flap. The blanket was removed. People crawled out one after the other. I had been sitting still. For me, the feeling was one of a personal awe and reflection. I crawled out before the shaman and I was awakened to an old reality by a blast of cold air.

"I now believe my experience inside the *Inepe* was a re-enactment of birth. To some indigenous people the *Inepe* represents the womb. When we are born, it is cold air that enters our fragile lungs.

"It was silencing my mind that brought a feeling, even in meditation, that I had never before experienced. I came to understand my own reason for being. For another two years, at full moon, I found myself there going deeper into who I am today.

"One evening, the shaman told me I was ready for a vision quest.

"So, now Don, you have a reduced version of my experience inside the *Inepe*. The exalted feeling became one of infinite oneness."

"Evie, I had no idea of the depth of *your experience*. I realize now that it may have started as an adventure, but now I know it was a spiritual awakening. Thank you for letting me into your world. I am honored."

A Pin Setter at a Bowling Alley

"Evie, you know, I am still digesting your sweat lodge experiences. I am amazed. You never talked about these things, yet they make you who you are. I also know about the various subjects you study. Yes am amazed!"

"Don, you make me smile! I suppose I am a soup that my parents made with the juices of their ancestors. For sure they gave me the desire to learn about myself, and everything around me. I continue to do so. These days, I am learning from you.

"Now tell me about the boy Donnie working at the bowling alley. How old were you? I know that must have been hard for a little guy. Also, since this is the era when Americans were smoking cigarettes continuously I wonder if your Chronic Obstructive Pulmonary Disease did not take root in your lungs while you may not have been smoking cigarettes, but inhaling massive amounts of tar through the smoke? I wonder if there has ever been such a study? I suppose the tobacco companies would not fund the research. One could spend their entire life investigating such fascinating subjects. I know I could!"

"Yes, I have no doubt that you would be very good at doing research of any kind. I take pleasure in observing you. What a focused person you are! Why did you go toward design and not science and research puzzles me."

"Don, with English being my second language, when I entered school in the USA, though I had papers saying I had a baccalaureate degree, I could not even ask where the bathroom was. It was a battle. Being of an artistic nature, I became a designer. I took an easy route. My choice was fine and paid for the things I needed and wanted. Because of this choice, I have had a charmed life. My constant reading of choice subjects gives me an outlet to follow that inquisitive part of me. What I read enhances my personal growth."

"Evie, nothing has changed. There is always a battle going on, just or unjust is not relevant here. Would you believe, when I was young the priests would bless the young soldiers on their way to war? I asked more than once if the enemy priests were also blessing their soldiers. No one ever told me what side God was on. Everybody was busy praying to one God but people were fighting and killing each other. When I asked my mother she reminded me again and again, '*We don't ask such questions.*' Anyway, my point is, there is always a lack of money in the lives of people who are poor, and some must become innovative in order to survive. There is, however, always enough money for wars. The politicians and the generals make sure of that. The public in all warring countries have one chorus. The chant is about safety and security. It has been so for eons.

"I had to be an innovative kid; the war effort did not help me or my family. Your upbringing and circumstances did not expose you to this kind of hardship. Your family, like mine, each in their own way, ushered resiliency. That's what counts in our lives."

"Donaldo, you are a man with a great deal of refinement. There is elegance to your mind. Do you realize how lucky I am to be part of your life?"

His crooked smile was adorable. Sometimes, I could almost see the boy despite his beard and moustache.

Let's Go For A Short Walk

"Okay, so you asked about the bowling alley. When I was in school the priests got the local newspaper. Once a week I got the old ones from school and brought them home. My father enjoyed them because he could read about what was going on all over the world. I was eleven years old, and I did not care about world news then. Yet, I knew our *Declaration of Independence*, dates of battles, who the presidents were, and a lot more. These things did not get me any money. I looked in the newspaper to find a job. I did!

"The bowling alley! It was about six miles from home. I can tell you I was a pretty determined boy. Six miles is not around the corner and Utica is not on flat land. The day came, when I went to ask for the job. After that walk I thought I was going to die. It took all my strength to open the heavy door of the alley. Once there, I looked around and the man with a tag on his shirt that said MANAGER became my target. I walked up to him and asked for the job. The war had taken almost all healthy men into the service, so the alley was hiring kids, none applied. The bowling alley was brand new and so was all the equipment. Everything was shiny.

I was a very small kid. Twice I said hello to the man, he ignored me. I pulled on his shirt. I asked for the job. He took my hand, looked at my fingers and told me if I could lift a ball and also pick up a couple of pins I would get the job.

"It felt pretty good, that afternoon. I think I ran all the way home. I worked there every day after school and on weekends for the next three years. Working in a bowling alley was a place where an eleven-year-old Catholic kid learned a lot about life. I became an entrepreneur. If there was some money to be made I found a way.

"I was probably the only nonsmoking pinsetter in Utica, N.Y. After a while picking up pins, I started picking up cigarette butts, sometimes I rerolled them, and sold them to the smokers, twenty for a penny. It was difficult to find the right paper to roll them. At the alley, I got paid six cents per game. I could make about three dollars on the weekend, and sometimes up to fifteen cents a week on the dirty butts. Saturdays were my best days, and I was there sometimes until 11:00 p.m.

"On Sunday, I was an alter boy. I never got paid for that. I changed clothes after Mass, gave them to my mom, and I went to work. Some of the bowlers felt sorry for me and sometimes got me a hamburger.

"Life was as good as it could be. My dad finally had a real job, so I could keep some of the money I made. I was twelve when I bought a shirt with my own money. Evie, it was my first new shirt. It was not a hand-me-down. I felt proud of myself.

"Evie, I must also admit I lived a long time resenting my father for not being able to provide for his family. Because in my family we did not talk about important things, I didn't know he couldn't find a job. I thought he was lazy. During that time in America, because of his infirmity, and also because he was not exactly literate, and also he was Irish, my father could only be a laborer.

"It was kind of like the circle for my father: bad leg, no education, no job, and the wheel kept on turning. As a child, things like that were not talked about in my home. I could only resent him because I didn't know why he couldn't work. These were difficult things for me to handle. I didn't know why he didn't work, and there was no one to talk to. In my family we did not talk about what weighted heavy in our hearts. But, you know what, life went on.

"Evie, I know I repeat myself. I think it is so I can digest what I am saying.

"On Sunday nights we all ate together because I was not working. It was very important in my family that we all eat together. My mother made white bean soup on Sundays, and sometimes when there was enough money, the soup had bones in it. It was pretty good.

"When I had enough money left after I gave her most of my earnings, I got her some corn flour. I once got her some butter. Something as simple as butter was a delicacy to her. I felt so good about giving her something she liked and missed very much. Evie, I truly loved my mother. The corn bread she made was the best ever. I don't think before I got the butter we ever ate any. Those were the things I resented about my father: he could not get anything special for the family.

"By the way, thank you for all the butter you buy for me. I like that. Your white bean soup is not there yet, but you know, it is delicious in its own way. I appreciate all the things you do for my pleasure."

"Don, you are kind, but please go on with the bowling alley."

"Well, the bowling alley was part of my life, a good part, but in the summer I had a different job with my mother's cousin. Her name was Ella. I loved her. She had a farm in Canastota, N.Y.

"From one day to the next, I was no longer a pinsetter, I was a farmer and worked on her dairy farm. Everyone worked very hard. We were all up at 4:30 a.m. and worked until suppertime. I learned to milk cows. This experience was in the early days of automatic milking machines. At the farm there was something exciting happening every day. I loved that place. I learned to empty the udders, which was a manual job. Cows could not have milk left inside them. It would go sour and I think the cow would get sick. I never really knew how, still don't.

Ella also required that after every cow was done the machine had to be cleaned and ready for later use. Oh, this thing that was done manually was called *hand stripping*. Farmers had many words no one ever used. That was one of my jobs and I did it well. I was responsible for stripping around fourteen cows, sometimes more. That was fun. Most of the milk went into a bucket, but I squirted plenty directly into my mouth. I became an expert. Not a drop of milk ever ended up on my shirt. You know, no matter how poor or difficult life was, I found ways to make everything fun. Today, all people do is complain about their jobs and expect things for nothing.

"I had another great job at the farm. I harnessed the horse to a dump rake and picked up the hay that was missed by someone else. When helpers were getting the hay, they made the turn to the next row too fast or something. A lot of the hay was not picked up. Something as simple as rolling hay was far from being an easy job. My father could not do that job either."

"Don, how could he have done such a thing with an infirmed leg? I guess you did not think of that. I suppose it is always easier to resent what people can or cannot do."

"I guess you're right. Every morning after I was done with the cows, I was responsible for picking up all the newly laid eggs in the chicken coop and bringing them to Ella. I never ate a raw egg. Some people did. I knew Ella made delicious omelets so why eat a raw egg.

"Ella liked me a lot, and when she thought too many weeds were in her vegetable garden, my next job was to pull weeds for ten cents a row. I swear, I believe some rows were a mile long. This is the only thing that was not fun at the farm.

"Since I was a businessman, Ella always smiled when she called me a businessman. She made this task worth my while. I also separated dandelions from the other weeds. She made tea with them and the handyman made wine or something like that.

"I don't think anything was ever wasted at the farm. Everything was used for something. I got a few extra cents and that was important to me. I was saving for a trip. My goal was to visit the entire USA by the time I was fourteen. Even then with no money, I loved this country, and I wanted to see as much of it as I could. A friend of mine was going to take that trip with me.

"Sorry for talking so much and for jumping around like the crickets you saw when we took our first walk."

"You are doing fine Don, your youth no matter how difficult was fascinating."

"Anyway, often after breakfast she had me go with the dogs to take the cows through three closed gates. I had to open them and make sure they did not go running some place else. There was a day pasture they had to go to get their food. There were no machines to bring them food. The cows were pretty free to roam. Evie, farm work is hard work.

"Before dinner, I would go out to the pasture and bring the cows back. They got milked in the late afternoon, too. The cows would take their time walking the few miles and they travelled at their own speed. Slow was their speed.

"The meals were always wonderful. Really all you could eat and all the milk I could drink. Breakfast at 7:00 a.m. Lunch at noon. After dinner Ella turned a radio on she had so everyone could hear the latest war news. I loved every minute of the time I spent there. During the Great Depression, when my father could not work and we could not stay in our house because we could not afford the rent, Ella Rockwell had our entire family live in her house. During this time my Dad worked doing everything Ella asked him to. In exchange we had a place to live. She gave him a little cigarette money, but he stopped smoking. I am glad I never picked up that habit.

"While we lived there my Mom did the cooking and some of the housework. Dad and Mom were very grateful to be there. After supper it never failed: the radio program about the war was on. We all gathered on the front porch. Sometimes, we listened to Roosevelt's Fireside Chats. Ella had lots of rocking chairs, and swings in the yard. I think we all learned to enjoy rocking chairs. Ella knew one song and we heard it every night after the program. 'You are my Sunshine.'

"I think she was singing this song to her dead husband who passed away. I am not sure when. His name was Frank. I don't know if we were related but my father felt like Ella's sister, Aunt Margaret, was like a mother to him. I felt Ella was like a grandmother to me. I did not like my grandmother. She continuously hit me with her cane every time I was near her. I am glad we did not see her often. My father's real mother gave him away to a Catholic orphanage.

"Evie, my father, was a child of the historical orphan train. Imagine that! I suppose this is what people did when they had children they could not take care of. Some people think it's fine. I don't. I know the result that abandonment had on my father. He was a broken man, without confidence. There were various organizations shipping kids all over this country. My father was in an orphanage and it was the Catholic churches that handled the kids and shipped them to be slaves on farms. My father, for sure, was one of those. I only once saw his back. There were lots of scars there."

"Don, you describe your father as a man whose life had been broken early on. I believe the scars you saw, left by his keeper, were not meant to be seen. He was a lucky man to have been married to your mother. I am always amazed at what humans do to humans."

"Evie, you are right. We were not the kind of family who walked around shirtless so seeing my father's back was an accident. We never talked about what I saw.

"I did not have much free time at Ella's, but when I did, I had a favorite room upstairs. It was loaded with antiques. This room was the closest thing to a museum I had ever been in. There were old newspapers, and letters from people I didn't know. This is where I found out that the farm had been operational since the American Revolution. I spent hours there as often as I could. Sometimes at night I would go in there to discover a range of things from old books to clothes. They even had a machine of Thomas Edison's first cylinder phonograph. I still get excited about all the things I was able to look at in that room. The good parts of my boyhood were molded there.

The Erie Canal

"Evie, you will never know what being without any money really is. Even when you had no support, and no money, you had education. You knew your circumstances were temporary. For me pictures found in a box were treasures and temporary escapes. I think this is why in my family people saved pictures. Let me take you on a tour of the Erie Canal after it was dug. Did you know they started this project in 1817 and finished it in 1825? It was America's first engineering marvel. To think that men with horses and picks, dug 353 miles of this canal is nearly impossible to fathom. Most of the ditch-diggers were Irish immigrants.

"You know, the Irish were not welcomed in this country. The Polish people had a hard time too perhaps much worst than the Irish. There were less Polish, at least in New York. In many places they would not hire an Irish man or a Polack. That my dear, is the way prejudice starts. My sisters said my dad had a sense of humor. I did not know that. He said the Erie Canal, where they hired Irish men, was where they learned to walk. They were all pushing a wheelbarrow in order to get some balance. I didn't think it was a funny joke. Regardless, the whole thing was a great success. Evie, life in America was hard for those building this country.

"I read in an old newspaper that the New York legislature authorized seven million for the canal project from Buffalo to Albany. It changed the face of America. Horses and mules pulled flat-bottom boats. In those, people could travel. I bet you did not know this expensive thing was only four feet deep.

"This canal allowed transportation of goods for a fee. Grain could be moved for $10.00 per ton instead of $100.00 per ton via wagon hauling. The canal debt to New York State was repaid in fifteen years. The canal was so successful it got enlarged three times.

"You like to read. I know you can find plenty of stories on the Internet about the canal. I recommend reading some. To me, these are the things that made America what it was supposed to be. People were not greedy as they are today, but that is another story.

"Evie, life may have been difficult, yet it was simple and good. Did I tell you, when I was a little boy, my Dad would take us Dailey kids down to see the large barges and how they managed to be raised and lowered in the New Barge Canal? I think I am telling you the Erie Canal was an integral part of my early youth, for sure after seeing all the pictures of every step of its construction, I felt it was special for sure.

"I know my kids teased you about me and historical monuments and buildings. Well let me tell you, my love for these things started there.

"The Oneida County Historical Building was another important building to me—just up the street from St. John's school. Again, when I had time, I was right there reading the history of Utica, Oneida County, and the Erie Canal. Most people who worked around these places could not get over how much interest I had in history. What they didn't realize is that it was the only thing I had been exposed to. Because of it, I have always wished I had majored in history, not pre-law. In high school when I wanted a class where I would get a sure A, I took a history class. Looking back I could say, this did not work too well for my degree in psychology or counseling, but ultimately I studied what I felt I needed to know about. In that respect, all was perfect! I guess like you, I knew I was free to choose the course of my life. I did make a few wrong turns."

"Don, we all take turns. Judgment calls them wrong. There are reasons for taking them. Some judge them as excuses. Perhaps, they are. I do not know. I can only judge my life and every turn I took got me to a place to learn about myself. I can safely say there were no wrong turns."

"Evie, are you still taking notes? I do talk a lot, but there is so much in this head of mine, a long life makes for storage of lots of stories. Let me know when you are tired. I must call the barber. My hair and my beard must be trimmed."

"I am getting tired and I must go get your medicines ready. Call your barber. By the way, if you ate something that would be great. All this time a coq-au-vin has been cooking. Yes, Don, there will be plenty of potatoes. I am giving you another five minutes."

"Alright, I will be quick. The Kinney/Rockwell farm was less than ten miles from the Erie Canal. It was like a museum complete with old firearms from the Revolutionary War, and with Indian arrows also. There was a lot on display in the great room. To be sure, I loved that old farm.

"I regret not visiting Ella one more time while I was in the Air Force. No one told me she was selling the place. I guess she had gotten too old to handle a farm. You see, when people do not talk about what intimately affects them, life goes on and memories get lost. I did not visit her, but when I became a successful real estate businessman, I flew Ella to Phoenix to visit us. My mom was delighted to see her again. She was 82 and it was her first time in an airplane. She flew back home and three weeks later passed away. I still feel a great deal of love and affection for her. I never told her how important she was to me. I wish the farm still existed. I would have taken you to visit it. I bet you would have found a way to make it into a bed and breakfast place. While I feel so much love for her, my only disappointment was that she had sold the farm before I could visit it as a grown man. She made arrangements with the buyers and she built an apartment in the area upstairs where that wonderful room was. Until she came to visit us, she never knew I had any interest in its contents.

"It's a good thing she never let me know about selling the place. I think I would have purchased it. Of course now I wonder what I would have done with it. I am not a farmer and being established in Arizona, growing a business in real estate, it was a good thing I did not.

"No matter what happens in life, although we refuse to accept it, everything is always in order."

"How very lucky you were, Don, to have been touched by such a wonderful lady. This part of your life was a lot more than about setting pins in a bowling alley. I am glad you told me! I still believe, the little person that you were, in an alley where there were mostly smokers, it could not have been a healthy environment for any one. Alas, at the time no one knew."

"Evie, for all the work I did as a boy, I feel it was the universe's way of preparing me to become an adult. I didn't stay in the box I was born into. When I used to walk the six miles back home after work, I think whatever thinking I did at that time must have expanded my consciousness."

The Child of an Orphan Train

"Don, you are on a roll with great stories about your family and you. You mentioned your dad lost his father at age four. Tell me more about that."

"Eveline, I think there were many failures there. I feel, the cultures that allow daughters to be married too young, and unprepared for life, fail their societies. This was the case with Irish immigrants. I know these arrangements did not serve anyone. Children learn from their mothers. In the case of my father, his young mother was not educated. She didn't even speak English. She married a widower with children, and had five kids in less than five years. My father had a twin. Evie, I am beginning to think like you—people have too many children and they rarely know how to take care of them.

"For most of my life I believed and rationalized that I was able to control everything. What a joke! I was wrong. Society has a way of promoting this fantasy and before you know it, the rug is pulled out from under your feet. That of course, is one way to learn about *not* being in control. In the case of my father, I think this idea is correct.

"So, let me forget about my philosophy. Let me tell you more about my father. I think this one is a lesson in American history. By the way, they did not teach about indentured servitude in the schools that I went to. They did not teach that young American kids were taken in indentured servitude, another word for slavery. I never studied about that, and I am sure in today's educational system, they don't teach any of it either. The only reason I know about it is because my father was a victim of this chapter in our history. It was not called slavery; it was for their own good that the Catholic Church sent the kids to homes in exchange for a roof over their head. The kids would work, no matter how young. My father did not talk much about that period of time in his life. I think the pain was greater than he let on. I had evidence enough from what he said, and what I dug up at the library, to put two and two together.

"Thank you, Evie, for the help you gave me when I was researching some of the stories I told you about. You helped me a lot. Not being emotionally invested is the key when doing this kind of digging. You are a good researcher. Thank you for taking me to the couple whose mother and father were also part of this indentured servitude group of people. They helped me a great deal.

"Most Americans don't know about the orphan trains, and when I think of it, I can't help but wonder what the Catholic Charities as a whole were thinking. They were an organization put into place to offer the love of God, yet they did not hesitate to put children on trains to be picked up by farmers to become their slave laborers. The kids did not sign any agreement, and they had no say in what was to happen in their lives. I call it slavery. I wonder if anyone knew the meaning of the word *indentured*?

"Evie, I still get angry when I think of these things.

"After lots of reading, I learned a great many of the kids were sexually abused. None of that was reported. Decades later some of the young men and women talked and some wrote about their experiences. The list of maltreatment is a long one. Some children were not given much food or clothes, and most never went to school. I have no doubt a great many psychological conditions decades later were a direct result of the treatment. Remember, I come from people who did not talk much about how they felt. You know, you helped me a great deal in that arena.

Thanks Evie! They may not have talked about it, but that did not change the scars.

"Perhaps during dinner, everyone talked about who they were. I bet you they did not talk about the fact that they possibly were the abusers of those less fortunate. As a rule people do not talk about the sexual abuse they are responsible for. The oppression of people is something I learned at an early age. We both know that will not change unless people become honest and aware of the wrongs they do.

"I imagine my father probably had nightmares about how he was treated. That is my speculation—we did not talk about such things."

"Don, often when I hear your stories, all I can do is shake my head; our upbringings came with a great deal of contrast. I believe, however, the progression in the human spirit has not travelled far. The prize in all this today is some of us have the ability to accept who we are. I think, all the flaws we encountered and how we reacted managed to give our lives richness."

"That's true. Let me tell you more about my father. Though I didn't always like him, he did teach me some great lessons. When I was young I thought he was too accepting of life's conditions. I felt that he was weak. It is a trait of young people: they think they know more than their parents for sure!

"I must give you some dates here in order to pinpoint this time in history. Thomas Joseph Dailey was born in 1887, in Philadelphia. Contrasting the poetic way you described my birth, I can only tell you he was born in October into ordinary circumstances. He had a twin sister they named Catherine. I think this is why my sister became Catherine. They were the children of Michael Daly and Mary Duffy Daly. Note that the last name was spelled differently. I never knew the reason for the change in the spelling of Daly to Dailey, but I am told it happened after my father became eighteen. He added the letters. Sometimes I wonder if it was to forget his father, who died, or was he just trying to carve a new identity? Like me he could have been a bad speller? I don't know.

"Michael was my grandfather. He was born in Ireland and came to the United States to work. As you know, a lot of people come here to work—usually they performed manual labor. I guess after a while he decided he wanted a wife. He went back to Ireland in 1884, married Mary Duffy, and brought her to America. She was sixteen, and like him, not educated. I don't know if she had *any* degree of literacy. At the time, matters of immigration were not important—people went back wherever they came from to get wives.

"The people from Ireland were not well liked. Come to think of it, any immigrant suffered the same bias. Ironically, this is a country made up of immigrants. The Irish were good workers, and I guess that gave them an edge.

"I grew up with my father always looking for a job. For a long time I kept newspaper clippings. Typically, ads from that time read: *Irish May Not Apply*. Things have not changed much, ads just don't tell who may *not* apply, but I can tell you, the unwanted do not get the jobs. The dynamics of prejudice remain the same: ethnicity, color, and religion. To that mix, you add Jews, and Latinos, and now Muslims. Prejudice remains the same no matter what the intolerance is about.

"My kids say I am prejudiced. I don't think so, but I must admit, I have not been exposed to a lot of people other than mostly the Irish. It was a special treat when your son-in-law from Persia and your brother, a Jew, and I were around the same table. Who knew that one day in my life I would be among the children of Abraham talking about the same issues?"

"Don, in this small planet, mostly because of religion and color, we seem to hate each other."

"Evie, what a complicated world we have made. I am glad you were from a society that was more accepting. *Your* prejudices look to culture and education rather than what we have been talking about."

"Don, I would say you are correct. I have learned to refrain from calling people peasants and ignoramus."

Let's Go For A Short Walk

"Mary, my grandmother, was sixteen years old when she got married. Their first child Joseph was born twelve months later. She got pregnant almost immediately after and gave birth to twins, my father Thomas, and his sister Catherine. Her husband, my grandfather, died in 1890, My grandmother was eighteen years old with three children. There were also the kids her husband had, no education, and no means of taking care of her children or herself, so she did what Catholic people did.

"You know, I now believe if people did a little thinking in life, they would seek education and they would refrain from having more children than they could take care of. In that respect, I feel I failed in my personal life. I did not make sure that my daughters were fully educated. I took the easy way out. My excuse was they did not express the need for a college education and I did not push. In retrospect I know that was a mistake! I think in raising our family the mother of my children and I were not the ideal models. Our children were loved, but children need a lot more. I know, I am not alone with that guilt. I made up for it by taking care of my mother, one sister, my first wife, and some girlfriends along the way. It's called mea culpa."

"Don, I suppose in your life, you did not realize that girls needed to be self-reliant and therefore educated. You took close care of wife, mother and sister. What I do not understand is that did not give you the incentive to have your female children educated. Well Don, that was indeed a failure in your life. You are not alone in your thinking. I believe many men in order to validate their superiority, think like that. To me, that is sick!"

"Wow! I didn't expect your brutal honesty, but you are right. That was the biggest failure of my life. I took care of people I didn't even know. I certainly had the means to take care of my daughter's education. I can tell you, I was very glad to know you didn't need me in any financial capacity. It was a breath of fresh air to know your home was yours. I must admit, you were the first woman I met who was truly self-reliant. At first, it was intimidating to be with a woman who didn't need me.

"You know, Evie, sometimes I think we should have kept your house by the creek. I don't know what I would have done with three acres, but you certainly had a very beautiful home. Come to think, ours here is the best looking home I have ever been in. I love it, thanks!

"You know I will stop talking when I am dead. Mary, my grandmother, was unable to care for her three children, so she placed all of them in a Catholic orphanage. As I said before, this is what was done in the Catholic communities of the time. That was all they could do. They had no means to feed them. Hard to swallow, Evie! I don't claim to know which is best. We all do things that are not wise in the eyes of others. I am old enough to know that every foolish or wrong thing we do has a lesson to teach us. Evie, I like the fact that we talk about our foolishness. Counseling enough people, I know most people don't know why they do the things they do. We are lucky to both have met our challenges. I also know that at times there are no alternatives, and a lesson must be learned.

"When I think of what my grandmother did, I get angry, but I also know she had to. Can you imagine—foreign country, no education, no family, and a bunch of children! All of us, at some point, either in complete denial or unawareness, caused great pain to others. That is the way of humanity."

"Yes, indeed, Don, it is the way of humanity."

"I wonder how most of the women and the children of that era reconciled their lives after such trauma. I know my father did not fare well. People did not go to psychiatrists, and they did not talk about what ailed them. To my knowledge there have not been any studies on the subject. I am sure if anyone did some investigating work on this matter, they would find a lot of malfunctioning people because of similar situations. I gave it some thought because I wanted to research these causes and their effects. My life had its own issues to be resolved and I knew that. If nothing else, after all the mistakes I made, I did learn to take care of myself. First and foremost, there was plenty of room to also take care of others. When we do not recognize or respect our own needs, we lose our power. By the way, as my caretaker, you must remember to take care of yourself first—Please remember that every day!"

"I do Donaldo, I do. Dear man, you tell me what is important to know. I appreciate your jabber. I learn a lot about human behavior from your stories. I even learn about my own behavior, and we both know I am perfect!"

"Eveline, you're fun to be around! You know Irish Catholic people had lots of children. Soon enough the orphanages became too full. A basket filled with apples, at one point, must be emptied or the apples will rot. That's the only analogy I have right now. There were many words used to indicate what needed to be done: *emptying out, clearing, and making better use of the space.* The overcrowding of rooms and hallways of orphanages became a routine occurrence, and the trains kept rolling in. No one ever complained, and the young mothers kept having more babies. Today, I don't think as an Irish Catholic. I have many silent questions. I wonder how my parents ended up with only three children. I know once my mother was sick. I didn't know what was wrong—she was throwing up a lot. Maybe she was upset since she was so sick. A lady came to the house. We kids had to stay outside. The next day, my mother stayed in bed. My father, who was not working, took us out. They never talked about why my mother got sick or upset. Today, I can't help but, wonder . . . "

"Don, most people have questions about their parents. We can choose the color of paint we apply to their portraits. The rest is not relevant to the love we have for them."

"Anyway, the children were taken to the station, and no explanations were given to those kids. This is what my father told me. Not a goodbye to his mother—after some research, I understood parents were not even advised—the children were put in trains and sent away to Catholic parishes where farming communities through the Eastern and Midwestern states needed farm hands. My father was one of those. He was four. The only person he had was his twin. All they could do was cry in fear, and hold each other's hands. He and his sister were separated at the first stop. The sister was taken out in Philadelphia. Tommy, four years old, was cut away from the only thing that made sense in his life: his sister. He was a small boy, and no one wanted a small boy. He was the last kid inside that train. His town was Constable, New York.

"Without his twin, this four-year-old boy was taken by a woman who came to get a much older boy for her husband. I can only imagine the fears and anxiety for this little boy. No child of any age is prepared for such treatment. Thousands and thousands of kids suffered indelible emotional damage. My father was not the only one. Part of the damage and trauma of his youth created his inability to utter what he felt about it and many other things, I am sure. Only once did my father talk about it. How scared he and his sister must have been. He said, when they took her away, she screamed for him. The priest at that station told him to sit-down and be quiet. He too was screaming for his Catherine. He said the voice of his sister always stayed with him. Maybe he did not hear his own voice."

"I am glad religion was not something important in my life. Of course, no one talks of the inhumanity of mankind, or that of their own religion. I am amazed, and have no words to express my sorrow, or perhaps my anger. How are you with that, Don? You too never speak about how you feel. You are the child of a man who obviously suffered such trauma."

His eyes swelled with tears that had to leave their source. Actually, we both had tears. The overwhelming emotions had to pass, on their own accord, while we held one another. I have grown to believe—sometimes no words are necessary.

"Well, Evie, sometime, I say that we are all born as a gift from God, but when I think of the life of my father, I have no understanding for the presence of God.

"My father, Thomas, was placed with a family that had immigrated to America from Germany. Jake and Katie Powell, were new owners and handlers. Jake spoke very little English, and instantly he disliked the young boy whom his wife had brought back from the train. He was too small, and he did not speak German. The day my Dad told me the story he was stoic, disassociating himself. He was the only child left, and had to get off the train onto the platform. Alone. Four years old. He wore a hat, and had a coat. I don't now what month or what season this took place. He said that he waited a while. He did not know what to do. He was very hungry. Mrs. Powell arrived. She took pity on him and took him home to her husband Jake."

"I wonder if in my life I will ever understand man's inhumanity to man. Nowadays I see pictures of war-torn countries—we can rationalize anything at all."

"Evie, it is demoralizing to know that as a species, we have the capacity for such cruelties, and yet we rationalize the whys. For the case of the Irish, since they were treated almost as non-people, there were no real provisions for their welfare.

"In the case of my father, for the next thirteen years, Jake treated him like a slave. They were, however, not called *slaves*. Jake would tie him to a post at the barn and beat him with his walking stick. If the stick was not available, he used a leather strap, which he used on the horses. He did not accept the fact that this little boy had physical limitations because of his size or age.

"His wife Katie, who had no children of her own, showed Tommy some care and love, but could not control her husband's treatment of the boy. She would put some ointments on the cuts on his back. And she repaired his shirts that where torn each time he got a beating. Jake allowed the boy to go to school, but not beyond the fourth grade, and not every day. His wife made sure that books were available to him when he was not working. My father said it was very rare that he could even look at the pictures in a book. If Jake saw him with a book, it was time to work.

"I think as a result, my father became an avid reader.

"He left the farm the morning of his eighteenth birthday and went to Philadelphia to try to locate his sister Catherine. It was the place where she had gotten off the train. At the time, when people were looking for family or friends, it was customary to post advertisements in the papers.

He posted a note and a relative of the people that had adopted Catherine spotted his notice and contacted him.

"His birth mother had remarried, and had reclaimed his sister Catherine and his brother Joseph, but not Thomas. My father cried when he told me not even his mother had wanted him.

"Evie, would you believe, my father went to visit his family in Pennsylvania, got reunited with his twin and his older brother, but never talked about his mother?"

"Don, I cannot imagine such a life journey. The human spirit is so resilient. Your father expressed a kind of bravery that is most uncommon. He was a brave man."

"Brave maybe. His instinct to survive was strong, but not strong enough to dissolve the scars of his past!"

"Don, as you tell me this story, I wonder, though you studied religions, what amazes me most is the gentleness of your character. You have a wise soul and maybe your father was more than a sperm donor. He imparted some kind of wisdom to you."

A Mother I Think of Often

"Don, you could not have told me the story of your father without telling me about your mother. I know how close you were to her, but I do not know much about her. So, dear boy, you better start talking. My computer is hot!"

"Evie, you're still willing to hear all this family stuff?"

"I would like to hear about your mother. From the little you told me thus far, I know she was a tender but strong woman. By the way, what you told me about your father was maddening, but also inspirational. At a young age he met courage head-on. Maybe he did not know it was courage or even balance of mind. I suppose in your life it was not only your mother who created equilibrium. That is a loaded word because it contains more than one meaning.

"You asked for it! My mother's name was Mary Loretta Mangan, and she was born in 1891 in Clayville, New York. She was a small woman and relatives called her Mini. So my mother and father were first generation Americans. Unlike my father, she was not a child from any train.

"I think my mother was the most pious Irish Catholic I ever met. She wanted to become a nun, but her mother, who ran a boarding home, would not allow it. She needed her helper. There was also the story that Mini was too sickly to become a nun, but not too sickly to work all day long in that boarding house. I heard that my grandmother was not too happy when my mother and father got married.

"Evie, often you told me that you saw me as a person who devotes his life to others. I believe my model was my mother. No doubt she dedicated her life to be of service to others. I don't know if that was part of her religious belief. Anyway, she married my dad since she could not become a nun. I have no idea if they were in love, but they accepted each other well. Her Catholic faith followed without ever questioning church, nuns or priests. Actually, my mother never questioned anyone she deemed a person of authority. Her doctors fell into that same category.

"So, you have a good portion of my roots, a bunch of Irish Catholics, who had a fair amount of babies and drank too much. I fell into that group. I am told when my father asked my mother to marry him she gave him a *conditional* yes. He had to agree not to drink alcohol. Since he did not drink anyway, it was not a difficult agreement to adhere to.

"Evie, there are things that are difficult to talk about. During the Depression years, lives went on, somehow. People survived out of will, I think. When one family had enough flour to bake bread they shared it with a neighbor.

"You told me stories of your father's sister in a Nazi Germany work camp. Having a French Jewish maiden name was not acceptable at that time. I know some members of your family knew what it was to not have enough to eat. When you told me the story of making bread with flour and sawdust I could not believe it, yet I read about it. I bet the children and grandchildren of your aunt know nothing of it all. I observed again and again, people do not talk about the things that were painful in their lives. I know this had been the case for my father. Based on what you told me about your *Tante Denise* the wounds are always too deep and too fresh, no matter the time. You already know about my parents not having enough clothes or food for their kids, especially me when I was born."

"Donaldo, you are right about family not talking about the throes of war. My aunt rarely spoke about being hungry as a result of being with her children who were in the work camp. I heard her only once, when I was at her home for some occasion. I think from that experience, they always had enough food to serve ten battalions. I was nauseated by the quantity of food, and I did not like any of it.

"Some of my cousins know nothing about their parents. One of the many I never met, after she read my book *The Canvas*, found me. She contacted me. She wanted to know what else I knew. What details I had left out of the book. They did not know that their mothers and fathers lived, for a long time, on one slice of bread a day. No one knew the first time I saw my relatives, four years after the war—granted I was a little bitty kid—they all scared me. I had never seen people who where so emaciated. It was when I was a bit older, that another aunt explained further the idea of wet sawdust in order to fill their stomachs. The sawdust was digested with great difficulties so they felt full. This branch of my family had digestive problems, which took many years to normalize. I cannot say if it is good or bad not to know about immediate stories in families, but for sure it creates gaps in global history."

"Evie, along with millions of other Americans out-of-work, my father was grateful when we moved to California. He worked for the Work Progress Administration for $15.00 a week. It was the most money he ever made. This, however, didn't last long because Congress gradually held back appropriated funds before WWII broke out. WPA work included the construction of public buildings, roads, parks, bridges, schools, hospitals and projects to provide jobs for the unemployed during the great depression. The livelihood of over eight million people depended on that. When WWII came along, those who could not make it in the army were out of luck. My father got a job at Remington Arms plant for half the pay, and he was lucky.

"I don't know how they made it. My mother and Catherine prayed a lot. She took in laundry, and you know there were no washing machines. I worked a lot, and I was told that we each had to do our part. Judgment was for God, my mother used to say. She was right in many ways. For sure, we didn't need to concern ourselves about the war because the generals knew what to do. I could not talk to her about that. She insisted the generals knew best. The fact that we were hungry was not to be questioned. I'm still working on that one because I think generals want war because they collect medals and their ego demands that. Besides, there is lots of money in war. In today's world I think there are more millionaires because of war than because of work.

"Don, so few know of your beginnings. I am not sure of the reason why, but I know you do not talk much about your youth. Sometimes I have heard you talk about the funny things you did, like diving into a small lake retrieving golf balls for money when you did not know how to swim. Which makes me think, people even do what is dangerous for their needs: for money, for food, and a lot more. Well, whatever the incidents in your life, you were molded to become a spectacular man. Who knows, maybe seeing high-ranking officers playing golf while people were hungry and dying may have altered your perspective on many things."

"Evie, you are very perceptive.

"When I was young I interpreted some qualities my mother demonstrated as weakness. Her kindness knew no bounds. I also judged my father to be less than what he was. I felt he was lazy, and that was why he could not find a job.

"I was an adult when I recognized my mother's ways were her strength. I also realized that my father couldn't find a job because of an infirmity of his leg. Having a fourth grade education did not help either. He was a man who read a lot, but that did not get anyone a job.

"I only knew discrimination about blacks and Italians. I didn't know Irish were also being discriminated against. My Irish father with a bum leg never stood a chance. No one ever talked about such things, especially during a war. Talking about personal life conditions would have been considered un-American. Poor man, he had three handicaps: the leg, no education, and, of course, being Irish. He could apply only for manual labor type work, those were the only type of work he could do.

"By the time I grew enough to understand how difficult his life was, without any self-esteem and not much education, it was too late. He had passed on. In all honesty, I don't know that we would have talked about his life's circumstances. I was too young and self-absorbed. I want to think if I had initiated a conversation, he would have opened up. I will never know.

"So, Evie, I understand why you often send people love and light. Sharing this with me has given me the tools and the reminder not to judge. As I told you, I judged my father. We all seem to judge people, places and things. We don't know why people act the way they do, and we don't know why their lives are the way they are, but boy we are always ready to judge them. It takes a lot of awareness and willingness to stop judging people. I am almost there.

"My mother, and also you, did some good teachings in my life. But now I really get it. I think this happens when we become aware of the impermanence of your own life. Anyway, my mother's religion guided her actions and you, with no religion, follow your inner guidance. In the two of you I find the same, about many things. Observing two women who did not know each other, of different backgrounds and so on, I find your cores are the same.

"So, Evie, now you know my mother!"

She Was the Mother of My Children

"Good Dailey, I know both your parents. Are you willing to tell me about your first love, the mother of your children?"

"Evie, I believe conversations between people spread the seeds allowing them to grow what is good. It is so in our case. I am grateful. I know there are no perfect situations, yet in our marriage, because of our constant exchanges, we continue to grow our seeds. We are able to grow minds, bodies, and souls. With death lurking outside my door, we have developed a great understanding of what life is: something neither of us has mastered in our previous relationships. This was the case with the mother of my children.

"Evie, telling you about my life with all its fragility and cracks, I must venture a few sentences about my first wife. Betty was an essential part of my life. Her life had its difficulties, but we had moments of great joy. I think in marriages we forget that the flow is not always constant. When young people get married they do not have a clue and only hormones control their lives. This was the case for us until our children were born.

"Look at us. Things change, things get renewed; our life experiences have brought us to that place where understanding and acceptance seem to reside. This is not the case when people are young. At least, it was not in my first marriage. Emotionally, I did not grow up. This a good evaluation. Too often we confuse emotional growth with financial growth. I did not know the difference.

"My wife was a kind and accepting person. Much later on I learned she was an enabler. I did not know that term. She put up with me taking in my mother and sister, my drinking, and God knows what else. I took her goodness for a sign of approval. I was dead wrong.

"The pathetic point is, I don't know if I drank because the marriage was missing something, which I could not name, or if I drank too much to escape the pressures I put on myself. Regardless, it took me years to know and accept that I had a serious problem and all I did was to make excuses. I did nothing to rectify the problem that in reality was a malady, a chronic one. I was irresponsible, in total denial, and that too I didn't know. Evie, travelling the road in denial and ignorance is dangerous.

"Too often we live a life of illusions. It was after reading almost the entire body of works from Master Subramunija who was an American Hindu born in California, that I began to understand a few things about myself. Finally, I had reached a point in my own evolution that I was able to realize for years I was waiting for a jackpot, a miracle. My ancestors had other ideas. The Irish bloodline probably made me susceptible to addiction. Ultimately, the choices I made were mine. For years I didn't know I was the one choosing. My ancestors had nothing to do with how many beers I drank. Later, after studying psychology to help others, I was able to help myself.

"At one point I had to shut the chatter of my mind and let my heart and my spirit direct what turned out to be a life that I have grown to love.

"I used to imagine myself in the space of an empty box. At first, I started to believe I was losing my mind. It is now almost ludicrous to think this was exactly where I needed to be. Inside that empty box, I had to feel my own emptiness. I had to become comfortable with all that I was and was not. What for years I believed was my reality was nothing more than my illusions.

"My wife put up with me but one day she had had enough.

"Evie, you know from your own experiences that development does not happen overnight. The more we want to know ourselves, the longer the time we must spend in introspective thoughts. There are many steps we must take to finally realize that our *self* is not our body. For me, it was like finding an old friend. It was not at all easy to find that friend, nearly impossible, and in the process I hurt some people. Of course, those we hurt the most are the ones we love, the ones that are close to us. Now the trick is while we are emptying ourselves of guilt and other matters, we must also live fully. During this journey, we accumulate bits and parts of anguish and delight. Those are the things that make us who we are."

"Donaldo, the more I know you the more complex I find you to be, yet it is all very simple. You engage my brain. Thank you!"

"When I was married to the mother of my children I could not articulate these thoughts because I didn't have them.

"I was ambitious and determined that my wife and children would have all they ever needed. For years I didn't know where this obsession came from. It took a while for me to find out I was reacting to having been so poor. My compulsive personality did not have room to stop and examine that I was being destructive.

"You know, Evie, I learned something else during this period of my journey. I learned that I did not have to react. I only had to act the best I could."

"Don, every time you open your mouth, I learn something. Each time I feel myself growing some. Keep on talking. I am paying attention."

"Evie, you are kind and comical too. I like the way you stroke my ego. You know I like to talk, so you may spend the rest of your life taking notes. During that first marriage, I worked a lot, and went to school, studying from pre-law to psychology. I followed my interests, which were many. To be honest, I know now, I did not give much time to my wife. Even though you say I am a generous man, I can tell you I was not always, at least not with myself. I gave things, but couldn't give of *myself*.

That's sad, you know! In my mind, because I gave her a house to live in, food to eat, clothes to wear, a car of her choice to drive, all was perfect.

"She had her own method to deal with the malfunctions in our marriage. The more money I made, the more she spent—and the more I drank. Remember the clock or the circle I spoke to you about? This is a very good example. The wheel kept on turning, but neither of us turned with it. We were stationary. We never talked about being dissatisfied with the state of our personal lives or our marriage. We didn't have the skills to enter such dialogue. We fought, but like all wars, there were no winners. Outwardly all appearances nourished the imaginary world we had created. To us, all was well because we did not know about communication or possibilities of happiness. We did not know what that looked like. We fed what was impermanent and broken, with illusions of stability. There are thousands of relationships like the one we had.

"It's that karma thing you talk about. We come here with things to work out. Some manage to work them out early in their lives, some don't. I think we meet the people we need to meet in order to grow. Mankind and religions decided that once married, all was to stay static. I am here to tell you when there is no exchange of thought there is no growth.

"Every so often she asked me for a divorce. At that time I was a very successful real estate broker with many offices with my name on the billboards. The people working for me, with whom I also did my drinking, would ask almost every Monday, *Is Dailey getting a divorce this week?* I was the joke and the joker."

"Don, I now have a sense of how complicated you made your life. I suppose what I call my chocolate addiction is a misnomer. Eating chocolate from Italy or Belgium does not control my life or hurt others."

"Sweetheart, it took a long time to realize I had to find the courage to be honest with myself. I don't know how it is for a woman, but I can tell you, it was the most difficult time of my life. The idea of divorce was just not going to happen to me. Of course I could not bring myself to believe divorce had happened to me."

"I wonder why men generally believe that their wives do not have what it takes to walk away?"

"I don't know why, Evie. Could it be that our egos are so blown up and out of proportion, we believe we are invincible? One day, my wife had enough of me and got that divorce. It was simple. She was done. At first, I could not believe it. We never discussed the reason she had. I knew having enough of something or someone was rarely the issue, but we did not talk about such things. In my stupor I forgot that I knew the reason. In retrospect, I must admit, I was abusing my wife. The scars she bore could not be seen, but I know she had them.

"Did I tell you before the divorce we attempted to find a religion that would give direction to our lives? I was honest about the dictates of a newfound temple. After a while, we both knew that the temple and all it contained did not provide what we were looking for.

"Evie, would you mind if I rest now? Thank you for giving me the space to express myself with honesty."

"Don, I know talking about such things can be emotional. We each must deal with life according to where we find ourselves in that clock of yours. I can say, conversations can happen when the psyche is ready. I believe we were ready."

He hugged me, and went to take a nap. I allowed the dance of understanding to penetrate the dark spots of my mind. There was light in that place.

I pondered a great deal about all that was said. The problem, as I understood it, was that they did not know what they were looking for, nor did they know how to communicate. I had grown sufficiently to know this to be the frustration in basic human needs. The magic of past orgasms did not suffice to satisfy the yearnings for an unknown yet empty feeling. The marriage, though fine from outside appearances, had deteriorated beyond repair. I have come to believe most divorces happen because of such dynamics.

When he woke up from his nap, he came to where I was writing my own book, *The Drum Made from the Skin of My Sisters*. As often he did, he stood behind me and he put his hands on my shoulder. He has a special type of massage he did, sort of acupressure. I could feel muscles losing their tension. When he was done, he said:

"Lets go for a short walk."

Eveline Horelle Dailey

Walking and Talking

There were two places for deep and valuable conversations. One was around our dining table and the other while walking around the lake where we resided. We did refer to it as *our* lake, but knew it was public space. When we were there, walking and talking, we did not see anyone. That was very good. We found magic in both places.

"Evie, do you realize our lives are comprised of one long conversation, and I think we have mastered the idea that the rules imposed by the mind have been released. What once held us prisoner, no longer has a grip on us. I like that! It's like a fish tangled in a fisherman's net—to free the fish you must untangle it from the net. I learned to dive deeply into myself in order to unravel what held me hostage. It was all in my mind all along. I was afraid of what I would find out about myself. It took me a long journey and I told you a great deal about that life journey I chose to take. To understand it, I had to release what was on my mind. Once I went through the opening, I found personal freedom. Only at that time was I able to walk my path. I came to understand that nothing was permanent, and it was between life and death that I had to keep score on my growth. Now I know there is no such need. Keeping score does not make us grow any faster. It does stroke our ego, I think."

"Don, I should go on an unending walk with you. Because of you, each step I take, I find myself growing to be better than I was before. I like that."

"Yes, the aim is always to strive to be better than before.

"Evie, as I've paid attention to myself, especially to my behavior, I've found answers everywhere. For a very long time I was blind to the universal answers. They were there right in front of me. I chose not to pay attention. It was easier to make excuses for the things that were not right in my life. I know now I am not alone in this approach to existence."

Eveline Horelle Dailey

Another Walk Around the Lake

Not too far from our home the lake provided us with tranquility—something we both enjoyed. Most times, our short walks took hours. Ducks and geese read our minds and answered the questions only they understood. I learned to listen while walking around that lake.

I learned to push the wheelchair we kept out-of-sight in the garage. A slight incline was sometimes a test of will, endurance, and tenacity. He knew when I asked him if he was comfortable that it was because I needed to rest on a bench close by. Like him, I had some limitations. Hardware that was in my back was often unforgiving.

"How about if we rest on this bench a while? We can see and hear the water fall and I will tell you about the circle we talked about a long time ago."

"Yes, the clock. You never told me much about it. I am all ears, but I did not bring a pad to write on."

"You will have to remember."

"You have a deal, Dailey. You talk, I listen, I remember. Do not mess up or I will push you right into the cold water."

"In that case, I will make sure not to mess up. I don't know about cold, but that water doesn't look clean to me. Do you remember when you were young you learned how to tell time, from a traditional clock, a circle? Most likely, you began at 12:00, or maybe 1:00 in the afternoon. By the way, in many cultures, this is where things begin. It's an opening, a beginning, a birth, something new. What I found is wherever you find yourself in that clock you are at a new beginning.

"The clock I talk about is not a keeper of time, at least not in the conventional way. For me, I visualize a clock as a way to indicate to myself where I am in my own development. The clock tells me who I am at any given time. I see the clock in four quadrants: First is youth and the teen years from 1:00 to about 3:00 in the afternoon. This is where immaturity resides, a place where I spent decades. After 3:00, in most cases, the young adult is born. It took me a long while to get there. I remained an adolescent for decades. By 6:00 p.m., the adult years had arrived, and in my case, I can say with some assurance I was not yet an adult. Evie, I think more than half of the world population is never trained to reach the various steps needed to get to adulthood. You know, in a few religions, and also in some cultures there are rights, some ceremonial rights of passage to go through. This is something we know nothing about here.

"I consider the best of my life to be *now*. You get the idea. I was a very late bloomer. I visualize the clock with the little hand around 9:00 p.m. To me, this is the time, sick or otherwise, that the end-of-life years make themselves known. Here and now Evie, I am there. Today, I can say I am a conscious man. I don't want to minimize who I am. I have been in that place for a while. You know, there is something freeing about self-realization. It took me decades; studies, books and you name it, to get to that place. I have come to believe that life has a beginning and an end, yet in a different arena it is eternal—another thing difficult to wrap my head around! This is a new feeling, one with a cognitive sense I can't always explain to myself.

"My sweet wife, it's getting windy. I am getting cold. Can we go home?"

"Excellent idea. I am ready also. I have to hurry and write these things before I forget them. You do know, Don, you give a lot to digest in one sitting."

"Nothing that a warm house and a bowl of ice cream will not fix. I know that our lives are difficult, but you have a way of making mine pleasant. Evie, I wish I could reciprocate. I have a great idea."

"And what is that?"

"While I am eating my ice cream put your new CD on and dance. There is something sensual and pleasing about how you move around the house when you dance. I enjoy it!"

"You know, Dailey, for a dying man, you have not lost a thing. I wonder if all men are like you?"

"I don't know, and I don't care. My life is sufficiently complicated to worry about the lives of other people."

Let's Go For A Short Walk

What Is the Time?

A day went by and we did not revisit the clock. We were gaining awareness each day; there was something disheartening going on physically. Lungs that do not hold enough oxygen have a way of impeding the workings of physical movements, including talking.

We had to take our lives *one day at a time,* a method he understood better than me. I encouraged him to go to a variety of Alcoholic Anonymous meetings. He was an icon in those halls where age and time of sobriety may have had something to do with being an icon. Few people knew of unbelievable accomplishments in his life. He did not go there to boast. He had two reasons to go. The first one was to give me time to rest. The second reason was to help those struggling with more than addictions.

At great length Don studied the work of Lao Tzu. I trust among the many ancient masters he studied, this one influenced him a great deal. We were both pleasantly surprised when we were *marrying* our libraries. We both held the same books of the Tao. He could quote Lao Tzu and tell me stories about the work of this philosopher who preceded our current era by at least six hundred years, or more. Don felt, Lao Tzu's self-effacing life rather than one of egotistical triumph was what he admired. I believe my husband followed this stance in his own life.

It was an honor to wallow in the knowledge Don accumulated in his life. He was a storyteller, but he did not let others into the space where he held his secret wisdom.

There were too many stories to hear. There was no time for bathing in pride.

"Evie, are you busy? I think I have enough energy today to tell you about that clock of mine. I gave it some additional thoughts. Back to the day's beginning right after 12:00 in the middle of the night when we are asleep, I prefer to see 1:00 as the beginning of the day. The opening to life as we know it. A birthing I could say. Here, what I tell you are stories my sisters told me.

"Around 1:00 in that cosmic clock I visualize myself as a young boy. It's a time for new adventures to grow from. It's the time as kids we have fun without ever thinking of consequences. That changes only when we do something we should not on such occasions, our lives change on a dime. We answer to parents, a teacher, or another adult who has our best interest in mind. Today the world has changed, and I understand even parents can't correct their kids. This is sad, you know.

"Nowadays there is not much of correction going on; we correct our dogs and cats while children and parents run wild and they are surprised when their kids turn out unfavorably. Now, because I have reached some sort of reason, I can look at life and know I acted irresponsibly more often than not most likely out of naïveté.

"I'll make it simpler. Look at the clock again as four quadrants."

"Don, sometimes you do confuse me. I think I need to digest what you just said."

"No need to stop. There is nothing to digest here. This is the way of life. So, 1:00 to 3:00 it's about the birth of new concepts, and new thoughts. Be it when we are young or as adults, we go through some transformation, which are all openings. We look forward to these spurts of growth, but often when they happen, we are not ready. I believe if I had taken the time to observe myself, to do some introspective thinking,

I would have arrived at some kind of balance. Now I know that was not my destiny. When we are young, our emotional vision is totally impaired. Again, I am not talking about a particular age. I discovered, toward the approach of 3:00, we think our parents don't know very much, or don't understand much, at all. It is actually when they could influence us for the better. Remember, I am talking about that imaginary clock, the one whose full rotation represents one lifetime. At that puberty phase of life, we reaffirm to ourselves that we know it all. We are young and have all the answers, and we know the rest of the world knows nothing at all. It's the time when hormones and ego control a lot of what we do. We think we are free individuals full of power.

"Something happened to me when I drank. Since I did not quite understand myself, drinking brought me the illusion that I was free of all unspecified troubles I had. In my mind, no one understood me. I had a lot of pressures. I was going to school. I was working. I was taking care of my mother and my sister. I had a wife, and soon two children to take care of. It never occurred to me that drinking did not solve any of the pressures I felt. I had no time to think. In all reality, I didn't know *how* to think. Who knows, if I had managed just a little thinking, many things could have been different. We had a marriage without much conversation about personal growth. Actually, we had *none*. I am not saying that was bad. It was just not part of our marriage. We were married not knowing what marriage meant."

"I believe most marriages exist the way you describe. I know mine did. Growth or personal feelings about anything were never discussed. There is a lot of emptiness in such marriages: a good reason for many divorces."

"I am glad we talk a lot Evie! I know I came from a world different from yours, and I am glad that you talk about what you feel. I like that about you. You are not afraid of exposing yourself. The mother of my children and I, we didn't talk about what we felt. I can tell you the first time I heard you with your kids, I envied your ability to be frank with them, although at times I thought they would never talk to you again, and five minutes later you were laughing with them. This must be something you learned early. You do not seem to hold grudges. And I am convinced that you look at all in life as gifts and lessons."

"Don, life is indeed a series of gifts and lessons. How else could we learn how to be human?"

"Evie, in my family, my mother, and my sister prayed for me, my wife cried, and the distance grew slowly. We were incapable of retrieving the illusionary love there was. I didn't know how to think. I also didn't know how to communicate my feelings, or my fears. Perhaps she had the same problems? I'll never know. See, these are all parts of various circles within the big one. Am I making sense to you?"

"Not completely because I have not been exposed to this sort of abuse, but I get the idea. I am glad I was not your wife when you were drinking. Come to think of it, I would not be tolerant even for five minutes about the whole thing."

"While life and work were happening, I was also walking within the circle of alcohol. It was a mess and no one ever talked about it. Evie, I believe, denying the obvious runs in families. Here I am talking about addiction, the circle of addiction, the shame of addiction.

"This I believe is how it begins: first there is the use—I did that in the military. Next there is the abuse—I did that early in my marriage. Only after that did addiction got ahold of me. Evie, I never told anyone, but I don't know if I drank too much because my marriage and the pressures of family were sometimes more than I could emotionally handle.

"Remember I told you the clock has nothing to do with how old we are. That clock measures our personal development. Mine was stuck at about 3:00. I had imagined some kind of fairytale, and that was not what I was living. I changed friends, and I became comfortable around those who drank. They understood me, although none of us ever talked about *why* we drank. Ultimately, I don't think one of us knew why we drank. Many of my friends had girl friends on the side. I did not. It took years, lots of schooling, and degrees I became very proud of. They gave me the understanding of what my addiction was. Like me, all my drinking buddies were hiding from themselves.

"Two more children were born. Evie, I can tell you, now I know I was not the best husband I could have been. I provided well for my family and I managed to convince myself that I was a good husband. We all can lie to ourselves. Most people do. When we are stuck around 3:00 to 4:00, we don't grow up.

"Looking inward from that place is impossible. We are not trained to go inside ourselves. Did you know there are countries now that are teaching children to meditate? Meditation teaches, without effort, to do some introspective thinking. When the kids learn to meditate, they learn to still their minds. I feel if more countries did that, the world would be a better place.

"The fact is, I was emotionally an absent husband. I married before I was mature enough to handle what I was getting myself into. No one talks to young people about that. I know it's a conversation parents should have early on.

"In our society we don't know the difference between love and sex. Young men generally think 'I am eighteen. I am all grown up. I don't know what to do with my life. I can go to the military a while. I can get married.' What they are saying is I am going to have a wife and going to get laid when I want to.' "

"Don, you have got to be joking."

"No joke, this is what most young man think about, and the girls, because that's what they are—girls— they want to get out of their parent's home, or they see themselves with a cute baby. No one knows the human value of a relationship and parents do not talk about relationships. Besides, when you are young, it's all about hormones. I also know that each person has a walk and a path to follow. Destiny demands it.

"In that clock, the hand can't go backwards. This is why I told you: whatever you do, you begin where you are. Did I say that before? Today in my life, I am no longer in that place of foggy mind and delusions. But I talk so much sometimes I forget what I already said. Do you think I have dementia?"

"No, Don, I do not think you have dementia. Besides, you had the doctor test you. You have a lot of stories, you have a lot of wisdom, and you talk a lot. If nothing else, it gives me a chance to take better notes."

"Evie, you are kind. I became a responsible man, of that I am proud. Again, we must be where we are in that clock. I could not go back and change a thing. But I often express how sorry I am that I made my wife's life some kind of hell, most likely the life of my mother, too. In accordance with AA, I did make amends. I also learned that what we do we do for ourselves."

"Your life and the life of those around you was perhaps an inferno. I know each of you had something to learn. It is the way of our existence on this planet. I find myself being grateful that I did not experience what you just described. Some clock you have, Dailey!"

"I have lots of stories about these times. I am glad you came into my life when you did. You are part of the stories. I will tell you more, later. For now, I am tired. You know when we expose what is emotional; there is a price, yet there is a release. You can say it is the price of personal freedom. Now I must rest."

One with Another One

While Don was sleeping, I began to examine numbers. I like numbers. Don was amused by my constant counting to four or seven—he felt no one did that. He knew it was my way of finding balance. In my life I noticed numbers everywhere. It was only normal that while he was sleeping and I was not, I would explore numbers, but this time it was only one. I was formulating my *one* sentence when I remembered how proud Don was, and baffled too, by my essay on thirty-three Chilean minors, trapped for sixty-nine days. To this equation, I saw series of threes. I saw the thirty-three bones of our spinal column. The sacred prayers repeated thirty-three times and so on. I too was proud when the editor of the Front Porch Review accepted my work.

This day I was only exploring a series of ones.

To make my cerebral adventure interesting, on that day the universe gave me a clue. I wrote it on my yellow pad. It was a *one*. Imagination took over and I began to think about a celebration at our home. The invitations went via the regular mail. On rather plain white recycled paper I wrote something like this: on the eleventh day, of the eleventh month, of the year twenty-eleven at eleven eleven in the morning we would celebrate with the aid of a glorious musician. I translated my jabber for my guests. At 11:11 in the morning, on the 11th month of

2011 we will celebrate. Silly as it was, I liked my exploration, 11-11-11-11:11 a.m. My mind offered me words to go with my many *ones*. On my paper, written in a circular manner: *lucidity, rationality, consistency, logic and reliability.* Examining my series of ones along with these words, I found no meaning to my mind's excursion.

While geometry may be a quest for reality, Pythagoras, the Greek philosopher, said: *"Number* is within all things!" Pythagoras wrote *number*. He did not use the plural in his sentence. He must have had a good reason! With this in mind, I decided to explore my theoretical statement. In my *one* mind, everything was fragmented.

A parade of ones offered my mind a pathway with no exit that I could see. There was something unsolidified going on. It was constant. It was illogical. If there was any lucidity to my exercise, I could not find it. I questioned what was or was not rational. I even gave a moment to my own sanity. Nothing at all made sense, but I wrote. It was a sort of exercise to entertain myself. Don often told me, I lived mostly in my head. He had a point.

What at first was cause for pandemonium demanded examination because something promising was happening and yet, I could not hold onto it because it was fluid. I only knew it was there. Had I stumbled upon a mystery not yet clarified? Plato said: *You cannot conceive of the many without the ONE. The ONE, is a principle able to put the universe in a single, complex form.*

Why did I not understand what Plato alleged? How could a single *one* be so multifaceted? Was I thinking of my husband and his many facets?

Lost in my analysis of *je ne sais quoi*, I decided to concentrate on the meaning of just *one*. Was I making complications where there were none? Was I losing my mind?

In time, Don woke up. After the regular breathing treatment, I decided to give him my new notes. He read, sometimes lifting his head to look at me.

Let's Go For A Short Walk

"Evie, you are not cursed to explore *one*. You are *one*, a singular person going through some horrendous challenges. You began your notes with one and one, and now consciously or otherwise, you realize that one will soon be missing from your life. I have a feeling you are exploring the force between sets of one? Yet you know there is only one feeling."

We often had great dialogue about things we could not change. This was perhaps such an occasion. I wanted to engage him one more time.

"I think as you were watching me sleep your mind used a symbol to allow you to differentiate in an abstract way the idea of eternal sleep and the fact that you will become a one."

"Don, at this time, this is not an adaptable reality, and I do not like what you said, not one bit. I also want you to know I am afraid because I have no control over what is going on now. I want to know how I will react when you are no longer *one* in my life. A conclusion contains within it the subtle mystery to enhance the creative power of the force of *one*. Was he talking about energy—what do you think? Whatever the man was talking about, I do not understand. I like the power we both exercise, two *ones*!"

"Evie, for the purpose of this exploration, I will take on your idea to a symbol made by the magic of the left-brain and its ability to count. All day long we resonate with both the negatives and the positives of life's energies. Yet it appears that energy does not recognize the differences. It remains energy, yours or mine. Just perhaps, with the energy flowing between each *one* of us, we could enhance the strength and the virtue to accept the things we can't change.

"Does that help you some? It is not my purpose or goal to bring pain to your life. Sweetheart, you're a person who understands numbers. You need to attach the divine in at least your number *one*. I am talking about the Oneness of God, the oneness of all that is possible, the oneness of all you are capable of and the oneness of the force within you. The oneness of acceptance for the things you cannot change.

"Evie, it took me a very long time to understand this idea. It has worked well in my life. I am hoping that you will find your strength as time goes by. You know this is a principle available to all of us. I have made peace with the idea of my one life on earth is coming to its end. You can do it, too, because you are a strong woman.

"I think I want something to eat. Later on we will talk more."

I left the room to get him something to eat. But I knew he had excused me so I could think, and grow to a place of acceptance.

The principle of *one* was indeed acceptable to me. What I wanted was the warm body of my husband never to grow cold.

Let's Go For A Short Walk

Half a Clock

Our lives came with plenty of joy, mistakes, and large amounts of laughter. To that there was a mix of frustration. This was such a day. I was to ponder about our last conversation. A boeuf bourguignon was cooking for Don, a carnivore who had lost his taste for blood. I used all the spices and herbs from Provence I had. It was cooked and ready to serve. To prevent any more *monkey chatter*, in my head I kept repeating, his taste buds will respond to good French food. In my usual way I repeated my new mantra four times. I would repeat the mantra four times, take four breaths and repeat the process. He was right. I was always counting, but not *one*. To appease the gods of the Irish he was also getting one potato from Idaho and carrots from our garden. Between breath and mantra, my mind kept telling me it made no sense that a neurological ailment such as Parkinson's disease would affect taste. My intention, and my food prepared with love, would reverse science. I felt it possible!

Covered with a new aqua colored cloth I had woven, I wheeled the hospital table in front of him. Once in perfect position, I elevated his bed, and the Bavarian China accompanied with silver cutlery and a white linen napkin made its appearance in front on him. Since the citrus were in bloom, I had collected some orange blossoms to render this meal somewhat special. I served him a portion large enough to fit on the palm of my hand.

We both looked at my arrangement and smiled. I had become an expert at serving food that would remain mostly untouched. I learned the art of acceptance.

He held my hand, kissed it, and smiled. He would wait for me to bring my food into the bedroom. Side by side, on top of the hospital table, we ate. Before such episodes—the short trip from the room, to the hallway, to the kitchen—tears flowed freely. I was also an expert at coming back into the room, perhaps with red eyes, but certainly with dry ones.

"I have a great dessert for you. I did not make it. It is a fresh Éclair from the German baker."

He took a few bites and pretended to like it.

"Evie, you go through a lot of trouble and work to create great looking meals for me. Thank you! I am glad you enjoy cooking. Remember when you are tired, that liquid thing full of vitamins is also fine and is less work for you."

Don was always attempting to make my life less demanding or difficult. He did not realize there was pleasure in pure anticipation. I knew one day, I would find the formula to bring back taste.

"Sweetheart, can we talk about that clock tomorrow? It must have been the sweet dessert. I am a little tired."

"Of course we can talk tomorrow. I will handle the dishes. When I come back here I want to take a nap. I am tired too."

I handed him the TV remote and brought the dishes to the kitchen.

When I returned he had made room for me next to him on the hospital bed. It was the place I occupied after dinner. A delicious nap followed each night as his fingers played with my hair. Our dog Charlie made himself a nest between his legs.

We understood that there was a great deal of gratitude to be had. We took time to accept life on life's terms. The fact that a clock was running too fast did not always matter.

If he said anything else I did not hear him, the grandfather clock struck 6:00 p.m. Don was not as tired as he said. He was in a talkative mood.

"Evie, you already know that my clock was stuck at 6:00 and it needed to be reset. That's the way I see my personal clock. That hour indicated time for growth in events in my life. Those were the various events that forced me to become a man. I recognized that I was a spiritual being, not a religious one. At that point I no longer had a need to explain myself to anyone.

"Now that I am good and old, I know I can't put an age to that place of awareness. I have seen young adults with that inner knowledge; they are successful in what they do because they are focused on themselves, not in a narcissistic way, but they seem to have something profoundly clear within themselves. I have also met people my age, so stuck in ways no longer applicable they can't extricate themselves from a barrel they voluntarily put themselves into. We both know this is all about fear.

"Have you noticed that in retirement communities such as where we live, it is *fear* that thousands of people identify with? The same applies no matter where people reside. Fear is fear. On the other side of the clock, if we are honest with ourselves, we begin to see what could be wrong with us around that 6:00 mark. The thing to remember in that imaginary clock: time is also an indicator that half of our lives have been lived. Like you, Evie, I too enjoy watching mankind as I am watching myself."

"Evie, humanity is flawed by delusions. Lives are addressed and lived like fairy tales. Look around—you will note, most people only exist because conception of self is mostly denial or fear based. All this becomes different when introspective thinking takes place. I think, in this context, we are doing just fine. Most people can't see the life as it is because for eons a world of misconception has been the way of being. I see that it's a phenomenon that exists in all areas of life. That mental place in the circle of the clock is around 7:00 p.m. We can't admit to our failures because that requires introspective thinking and we don't know how to think.

"Evie, I hope I am not boring you with what I am saying?"

"No, Donaldo, you have me listening attentively. I just realized I need a tape recorder. Sometimes what you say requires digestion and I do not want to distort what you say."

"In that case I will continue. In our lives we are fortunate enough to analyze our wrongs with honesty. The hard part is, as you know, we must find the courage to change behavior instead of blaming others. It's never about others. Evie, we also know without support it is difficult to achieve changes. We also know it's not impossible. I did it reading, going places and learning to find myself. I think also in AA having a sponsor created that pair of safe ears to talk to. It's good to get somebody else's perspective."

I stopped him for a moment. My fingers were tired, or perhaps I wanted to do more than write words? I wanted to digest them as well.

"Evie, in your garden, there is a time when you can tell just by looking if a plant will bloom and bear fruit. The plant knows if it has some blooms, it will do what it was meant to do. We humans are complex. We tell ourselves that we are great and perfect, and we become blooming idiots—people know, but are busy feeding themselves illusions about being in control. Most don't do the things they need to do to improve their lots.

"You know, Evie, during the worst of my life, I absolutely believed I was in full control. My mother, my wife and some friends could see the downward spiral I was in, but most would not talk about it. That's part of the way we function: if you don't talk about it, it will go away. There is also the possibility that they knew they could not do a thing about it. I don't know.

"When we are immature, and by the way, age has nothing to do with maturity, we don't know that we are choosing a wrong path. We think we are invincible, so there is nothing to be told. I think men more so than women believe they have the key to everything.

"Evie, How about a cup of tea? I noticed you did not have your computer. Looking at your handwriting, you'll never be able to read what you wrote. Is something wrong with your computer?"

By the time he ended his sentence, I was in the kitchen about to make two cups of green tea.

Eveline Horelle Dailey

Three Quarters of a Clock

Two cups of tea and one Irish cookie—we were happy and predisposed to continue our everlasting talks.

"Evie, let me tell you, from 6:00 to 9:00 p.m. you either wake up to what is important or spend the rest of the time inside the circle adrift with no particular direction. You can float like that until you die. Millions of people have an under satisfied life or they reside in a no man's land, and they don't know how to get out. With no fulfillment in life, there is only a stationary position that presents one disaster after the next. Some drink a lot, like I did, and some do not. I drank, most likely because I was afraid to look at myself. By the way, Evie, most of our bad behaviors, I think, are fear-based. Humanity likes the status quo.

"I remember when I was a young man, in the Air Force, my job was to look for Russian airplanes. At that time in our history, we were terrified of Russians. They were Communists. That by the way, is a word that scares the entire USA. Without understanding of what a communist was, we were afraid of them because we were told we needed to be scared. They spoke a different language. They did not have a melting pot on their land. They were not a democracy. I know in my lifetime, we will not trust them. People of this nation do not make attempts at understanding what we know nothing about. I must thank you, Evie, I realize with your openness, I am learning people are people no matter when they come from. Governments, is what we need to be scared of. Theirs and ours!

"You opened my eyes toward places I would never have looked before. When I realized you had friends in Russia I was concerned. Old tapes were playing in my head. As you say often, we are groomed to think one way or another.

"Not too long ago, I met a guy. He was brilliant, perhaps a little rough around the edges, but that's my opinion. By his speech, I knew he had a lot to offer. Very few people talked to the man. He was different. He was Chinese. Like you, he has an accent. My guess is, since the majority of the people didn't know him, they didn't trust him. We do the same with Blacks and also the Hispanic population. The Chinese and the Japanese have experienced some cruelties in this country. The point is, some people are good and some are rotten. No race escapes this phenomenon. It took me a long time to grow enough and simply *accept* this as a fact. How come I never heard you talk about friends in China? I know you cover Europe and the Caribbean with plenty of friends. Japan has brought you some good experiences. You are lucky. The Middle East gave you content for the last book. Gosh, Evie, you know people from all over. By the way, I like the Russian art you've been showing me. When you wrote *The Drum Made from the Skin of My Sisters,* I realized one thing: you are not afraid of people. You see the differences, you ask the questions, but you are not afraid of them. You were not groomed to be afraid.

"Some of us of the human race are programmed to fear what is different. This is why when you were in Georgia, and attempted to work with some hotel owners, your accent, and your looks made you a threat to them. Calling you a Communist from New York showed their ignorance. I am certain the people around that boardroom table were all rich enough to own hotels. When you told me this story, you reminded me of the abject ignorance of people. As an American, I was not happy to hear that."

"Don, in case you forgot, I chose to become an American citizen. I can tell you that day in that room with those idiots, I was ready to get my flag back."

"This brings me back to what we were talking about. In my case, success in business did not change the fact that I was dissatisfied with who I was. I was self-centered. The life I carved for my family and me did not fill the emptiness that was created with the hazy view I had had of myself. It took no time to get to the next level—alcohol abuse.

"Now I can admit it; for years I was too fearful to change my own behavior. I wanted the world around me to change. I think this is why people do not change how they conduct their lives. The complexity of what we do to our selves is mind-boggling. An ounce of honesty can assist anyone to climb mountains.

"When I told you I did not like who I was, if I had to place that time in my imaginary clock, I would say it was about 6:30 to 6:45 p.m. For me it was the time to wake up. One moment of despair, one sober instant, and my life and everything changed. My perspective shifted. I am lucky because I found guidance. I changed direction.

"I read a multitude of books, and changed friends. What once was important lost significance. It's during this time of my life, while searching for I am not sure what, that I found my own truth. It was a long journey to find my truth, and it continues to change as I grow. My truth requires that I do what is best for me. Once I do this, I can turn around and do what I judge is good for those I can touch.

"What's odd is that I always knew this truth, but I was afraid to change directions. I was stuck!

"A little after 7:00 or so, I believe I was on my way to becoming a human being with a conscience—a person I now like every day.

"I am only sorry that I did not meet you earlier. Life has prepared us for our union and taught us how to communicate. I needed that. I still do! Now that I am close to 12:00, I wish I could explore life's many more allegories with you. How about if we continue to talk about all that later? I am tired. I am certain, you know, when we talk about what is deep inside our souls, our bodies get tired. Ego does not like that, so the body reacts. Even if I were not sick I still would get tired. Laws of the cosmos!"

"You are a patriarch, alright! Your life did not seem to unfold like the average bear. I want to hear more about this clock of yours. Your concept is fascinating and makes a great deal of sense to me. I want to know how you woke up. When did you know you were on a journey? Who are the people who guided you? I want to know every morsel of your life —I want to feel with my bare feet the path you walked on."

He had a way of looking at me that always made me smile. Each time I felt he was saying something like, you silly girl!

"Hey Dailey, were you on that endless walk when we first met? Was that walk part of your self-examination, or was it an examination of me?"

"I know you demand a great deal of yourself, but has anybody ever told you, you demand a great deal of others too? Not all people operate as you do, Evie. We will talk about these things later. Yes, I was examining you and also me. We were walking the same path. I told you already. I am tired."

I looked at him and smiled. A piece of me knew what soon would be missed. I pondered about his zenith on the clock.

I held his hand. Was it for his benefit or mine? A question I know I may never answer with certainty! It did not take long, and between the large numbers of breathing treatments we talked more and he slept more. The routines of our lives had changed without announcement. In gratitude, we both bowed to the demands of his body.

I was no longer angry.

A moment later, I left our bedroom. In front of the hall mirror, I looked at myself. I had been dancing with denial and also attempting not to escape.

It had not been long since we discussed the reasons for the need to rest. I guess he was right. The body needed rest. The mind and the emotions suffered without it. Diversion in any form had become a survival mode that no longer worked. In both our worlds of illusions we had managed to fool ourselves. Humans have a way of coming up with reasons and great excuses. We were both experts.

Our lives had been busy always. Now we added intensity. What the body could not do, the mind had to find resources and modes to accomplish.

Soon, body, mind and spirit joined us in conversation. We understood the need for space between us. Only individually could we process all that we were. He once told me he had never met a person so open to the world yet so singular as an individual.

I knew at the first steps we took towards the source of Montezuma Well we were culturally different. In the quality of our relationship, we were actually very similar.

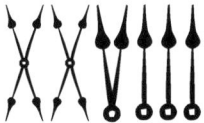

Living in the Now

I heard him cough. His was the signal to begin yet another breathing treatment. I became an expert at recognizing the needs of my patient. Because I had a daughter born with asthma, I knew the sound of a cough that came from a person in need of oxygen—a particular sound with a metallic noise I could recognize even if miles away. That sound also affected my demeanor.

I was amazed by my own capacities as a caretaker. I learned to identify the range and implication of this tinny sound. There was a difference in the need of pounding on the back of the chest versus giving oxygen.

As I prepared all that was needed, I remembered the first time when the oxygen was delivered to our home. The law demanded that on the headboard wall, over the bed, a sign with large red letters "OXYGEN IN USE" had to be affixed. Anyone entering the room would see it. That sign petrified me. It symbolized a type of defeat. Soon enough, preparing tubes and nosepieces, I no longer had time to pay attention to that sign. In no time, the panic of insecurity left me. I knew what I was doing. I wonder now, how fast we humans become anesthetized to almost anything.

"Donaldo, while I was handling your mask and the oxygen, I made a discovery. I was thinking of the day this equipment was delivered. It became obvious to me I was not living in the *now*. As a result I could have gotten us blown up. I wonder how many accidents happen because of momentary unawareness?"

"Evie, you need to remember that you are a human being, trying her best to help another. As much as you would like to, you are not a sage, and therefore, living in the *now* may not be something you can do *all* the time. Come to think of it, I know the monks I was with in New Mexico often talked about the simple things that took them out of their meditative mode. Learn to forgive yourself of the little things, and the big things that require forgiveness will follow. We give too much importance to insignificant matters. Just don't carry these things because the load will get too heavy.

"I feel elated to know you are human, Evie! When you told me about this *now* business—remember that first walk we took? I thought of Emmet Holmes of *Religious Science*. He was a teacher able to bring awareness and mentorship to those who studied his philosophies. To my knowledge, he was one of the first Western teachers to talk about living in the *now* as you strive for in your life. The ideas of mysticism, and metaphysics, got me to the spiritual principles for living my life within my own truth. I learned to express God as I am continuously able to understand and grow from. What he was teaching gave me tools of understanding of the great mysteries. I am still a practitioner of *Religious Science*. Like you, I was touched by great minds.

"The philosophies of this man and many other teachers talked about living presently. He talked about being where you are. He insisted that in order to succeed the need to focus was important. He often reminded his students, *now* was not so easily achieved.

"Evie, when your back hurts, I use all the methods I know to help you heal yourself. I must align myself to *divine energies*, focus, and be present.

"So, Evie, you were doing a breathing treatment for me, and thinking about the bed and the oxygen. Dear, you were not focused, that's all. When I do a healing treatment for you, I invoke all the methods I know. Sometimes I get lost in them. Evie, we sway in different directions because this could be a cosmic process to remind us that we are human. The man who influenced my many understandings was Gurdjieff. Not always easy to understand but one to digest. He got me to an opening.

"Evie, I know you were brought up to believe you were perfect. I try to live my life with the awareness that life can only be lived in the *ever present now*. In other words, like when you talked of your steps, one moment I am here and now taking the right step, the next moment I am not and sometimes I fall. I do not like to use the word *always*, but I know there is always another *now*. Through Gurdjieff, I understand you."

"Dailey, you have a way of giving me examples that puzzle me and send me searching for more. By the way, of course, I am perfect! I know I told you so a thousand times. Perfect, just like you, searching to be better, better than before."

"My dear Evie, the only concern here, when we are busy thinking of one thing and doing another, we are not being true to what we are doing, and we are not being true to whatever we are thinking about. When we do this, which consists of probably most of our waking moments, our intentions to be in awareness are not met. Ultimately, we are not true to ourselves. I try to be true to myself, the best way I know how.

"There is something great about being on the journey that we took together. We took time to think about taking the first step. When I spent that long season of my life at the Grand Canyon this is what I felt. There was perfection to each step I took. I can tell you, and I am sure you understand. For me, there is magic in that place."

"Don, I think we are both fortunate to have arrived at a point in our lives when we are capable of deciding to live the way we see fit. I know for me, this decision enhances who I am. I know this to be the case for you as well. I cannot imagine my existence any other way. I have a great deal of gratitude because I know you understand where I am. It is not clear where that journey will take me."

"Evie, the mundane things are no longer important in my life. Who knows, it could be why the word *mundane* was invented? As I get older I understand the idea that I give my considerations only to that which interests me. When nothing is important to me, my mind falls back to my yesteryears and focuses on the past and that is not a good place to remain.

Move Away from the Past

"I used to tell my employees, and the patients in the recovery center, *it is fine to visit the past, but don't stay there.* There is nothing to be gained by living in the past. I know when I am in that other place called the past, whenever that is, I am not aware or have a clue about what is in front of me. I am not telling you anything you don't know. It's about your *now* thing."

"Don, you tell me wonderful anecdotes. I remember you telling me when I mentioned *now* during our first walk. You told me that I got you to a window with a view. You just opened that window for me. How fun. We now can look through the same window."

"Evie, the thing is, we are products of our past, yet it is up to us to change course when we find the past does not serve us well. I believe there is nothing that can't be accomplished if we practice the philosophy of AA: *One Day at a Time.* You have to admit, in principle it is simple and easy."

"It is a great organization. I may not be a member of your club, but I certainly enjoy its fruits. I wish there were organizations using the same principles to assist non-addicted people in search of improvement within their lives."

"My dearest wife, during that walk you talked to me about a few things, *now* was one of the many things that alerted me that our friendship would grow. I didn't know right then that we would be married. I guess that was up to a higher power in both our lives. Evie, you made a good choice and I am glad you suggested we get married. My children do not know it was your suggestion. Funny! Actually, they just don't believe me. I knew you were not the cohabitating type. A woman as independent as you rarely has a desire or a need to have a man around. I can tell you there is something very refreshing and also challenging about that. At the beginning of our relationship, I could never tell whether you were coming or going. Now, I am very proud to be your husband, even if it took you five years to get the name right. I like the fact that you are independent."

"You are kind, Don. I know when people get married the wife takes the husband's name. Something I feel is ridiculous. I did not change my name for many other reasons. For over twenty-five years I had my own business. The company's logo began with my initials HE for Horelle Eveline. That HE belonged to my father. My attachment to him and the name he gave me had ahold on who I carved myself to become. The idea of changing my name and the name of my business was more than I was willing to do. I am glad you are a man whose strength of character was not intimidated by a name. Yes, it did take five years to add your name to mine. I now enjoy who we are together."

"I had to put my big boy pants on when I had to face the fact that you, on some level didn't need me. For any man, this is a challenge because our ego wants to think no one can be perfectly fine without us."

"I never thought about that. That is true. I took care of my life, my business endeavors and myself. I have grown to need you. So, dear man, you are needed. You can relax."

"Anyway Evie, with all the studies I did, *now* was a significant point. I think the greatest accomplishment of my life was to open my consciousness to who I was becoming and to who I am today. I can make choices based on the acquired truth about myself. Of that I am happy because I was not always in that place."

"Dailey, it is such an honor to walk side-by-side with you. I like that place where you are now. Having many diseases does not determine who you are. I like that."

"These days, as I have plenty of time to ponder, I can appreciate each moment granted. Sick or otherwise, I have thankfulness for right *now* and right *here*. Today, I know the meaning of being thankful. It's more than a word. It's an action. You will never know what a gift you are in my life. I am glad you decided not to leave me. But Evie, when I am gone, remember that you have plenty of life left in you. Live fully for each *now* you are granted."

"Don, I so appreciate the depth of our conversations. Being conscious today, I cannot say I was always cognizant of what consciousness was—I thought I did, yet to arrive at that place of recognition I had to intentionally will myself to grow up. Based on findings that came along the path I took I know I will live as fully as I can for as long as I can. I will miss your essence. Few men, I think, arrive where you are: that place of self-truth is not easily attainable."

"Evie, I spent years without awareness of my surroundings. I'm old, but conscious. God, I don't know how I would handle life with my mind completely gone. Well, I guess I wouldn't know. It must be hard for all concerned when that happens. People I know with family members with dementia or Alzheimer's have hell in their lives. Yet, as you do, many take care of the ones they love."

"It breaks my heart. You care for me without ever complaining. I know I am a patient with many demands on you and I also know about your back. That, my dear, hurts me more than watching myself slowly die."

"Don, do you know why I see you as a patriarch?"

"Probably because you have some silly conception of what I'm not."

"No, Donaldo, it is because of the roads you chose to walk on. You maneuvered great obstacles and gained experience. The self-discoveries

and the studies you devoted time to make you a rare jewel. I witness every day what you do for others. The person you are today is remarkable. The wisdom you have accumulated and share for the benefit of others is unprecedented. I now know this is the *better and better than before* you spoke about. You are indeed better than before. I have watched you with others and also with me. You take your acquired knowledge of things unspoken, and point others in areas that will improve their lives. You certainly do it for me, too. You point people toward systems of personal awareness and growth. In my case, there has been a great deal of growth, and it unfolded an understanding of the nature of what great love and internal harmony I am capable of. Those are things, in my eyes, not only making you a patriarch, but also a wise man. Know that I do not put these attributes in any order.

"Don, not all people can do the things that will make them better people. In fact, I feel most people are petrified to change anything in their perceived comfort zone. This is why battered people remain in bad relationships. Men stay with the same job they hate. Teachers who have been schooling with outdated material cannot prepare students for the world they will encounter because they are too afraid to initiate changes. I became closely familiar with this dynamic when I was writing *The Drum Made from the Skin of My Sisters*. Individuals must be motivated to alter their way of existing. I witnessed many times that you have the ability, in the subtlest way, to motivate people toward the changes they need to make in their lives. You show people that there must be communion between the different aspects of who they are. You teach that, my man, by example!

"In my eyes you are a Patriarch: one human being, head of a family, and also a greater family at large. People look up to you, sir! You are one individual to learn from! Know that I do not use the word patriarch in a biblical manner. I do not know enough about the Bible, but I know a patriarch to be the head of a clan. I use the term to describe what I call *Pater a familias*. In other words, you are the father of the family. Imagine! I do remember some of the Latin I had to learn!

"So. Yes; you are the father of the family. I also believe you to be a father from long ago ancestors, and you arrived at a place of balance. That, dear man, you teach well all day long from how you handle your life and the choices you make. I never heard you talk about this aspect of your life. You may talk about the good time you had buying and selling houses, but I believe most people do not know the real you because you do not boast!"

He looked at me with a puzzled smile—which felt good, because he knew from what place I was finding my passion.

"Furthermore Don, no one can take away the accumulated knowledge you have acquired. I am not blind to the fact that arriving where you are demanded critical introspective thinking. I know of the drastic inner changes you had to make. I know you did not become this man by osmosis. Yes, I can call you a Patriarch any day of the week."

He looked at me again, and in a pensive manner said:

"If in my life, if I accomplished what you say I did, or touched anyone in a positive manner, I accept the responsibility that comes with the title."

Words he spoke often propelled me right into his arms. After a while, when I broke the mood of physical love, we resumed our dialogue.

The Essence of the Ancestors

"Don, I witness that you are a man without any entrapments of ego. Your essence permits you to release the suffering of many around you. Just thinking about it, I can feel my chest rise."

"Evie, I am glad you see humor no matter where you turn your head."

"Don, without question, I know the package that you are, and it is a gift the universe reserved for me. I am cognizant that you exercise spiritual ideals based on your own convictions. I like that a lot! In the condition and circumstances of your life and mine also, to continue to watch you and me becoming who we are is a model I know others can appreciate. Of course, if they choose to Mr. Patriarch, I walk in gratitude a step at a time in your shadow or by your side. I am learning also to be better, better than before."

"Evie, I love the things you say about me, but I have learned what you judge to be great in me came from what I have read and exposed myself to. I have no idea how people progress emotionally and spiritually without guidance. I am not one of those who learn by some kind of nameless absorption. I have plenty of guidance, and you would think at my age I wouldn't have mentors any more, yet I do, young and old. I learn all I can every day. The problem, I think, is that most people are afraid of guidance because they feel they will lose control and most of all they may have to change in order to find peace of mind. For instance, many of the people I counseled were in a self-imposed ocean where drowning was the only path they saw. The sad part is that they often refuse the idea that they had power, untapped power, but power just the same, to change whatever they wanted."

"So, Don, the difference, as I understand it, is that what you were exposed to and what you read, penetrated, was digested, and became part of your core. Do you know most people are not willing to do any of what you did to achieve the person you are today? Besides, it is easier to blame people, places and things for everything that is wrong in life."

"Something like that. Fear is powerful—we both know that—and too often we remain static instead of becoming fluid and pliable. In other words, we are afraid of our part that is our God self. We are too often afraid to reinvent ourselves. I found the road to my peace and harmony in books, and in great teachers, but I had to walk the walk as they say.

"I know you've read him, but among those I found to be influential to my life, I say Viktor Frankl was of great importance. His Logo therapy is something that served me clinically with the patients I attempted to help. Personally, when I was drowning and in utter despair, I found hope in his work. Later on, working with people suffering from psychogenic neurosis, I became aware of their turmoil, and began to understand them better. I was able to help them. The other person who influenced my thinking, was Father Pierre Teihard de Chardin. He was a Jesuit priest, a trained paleontologist also. In his book *The Phenomenon of Man*, he said that it was in our uniqueness that evolution was enabled. He got into trouble with the Catholic Church. His liberated mind and his studies took him to the crossroads of science and religion. He understood the human potential. His philosophical writings got him banished to China. There, he and Davidson Black co-discovered the Peking Man-fossil back in 1934. Both men understood the intellect and spiritual nature of humans. Both men understood the reason for being.

"Evie, it is hope that keeps us afloat. I should have met you over twenty-five years ago. What a great time that would have been. I feel cheated because our time together is limited."

"Don, you are simply amazing. I did not know you had heard of Pierre de Chardin. Most Americans have not a clue of this man's work. I did not even know that his writings were translated into English. You know his research on the human spirit took him all over the world and got him in plenty of trouble. His findings were opposed to the teachings of the Church. For long periods of time he was exiled. I know that the body of his works was over five thousand pages, and like you, I read it."

"Imagine that. I even know about Victor Hugo and Jean-Paul Sartre too, Evie. Did you think I was an ignoramus?"

"Ignoramus you! Not a chance!"

He was glad that we were crossing borders. He was always conscious of our cultural differences, and when such things happened both of us felt a rapprochement of culture. Ultimately, we were just people speaking with different accents.

"Back to Frankl. You do know when a person has lost reasons for being him or her soon dies. Frankl, found that those who survived the atrocities of the death camps in Nazi Germany who had found reasons to live. They had hope. My belief tells me when we have hope, the universe responds accordingly. We become invisible to those about to hurt us, and visible to those able to help us."

"Don, are you reading my mind again? I very much believe that my own life seems to operate from that wave. When I believe this idea, I am open to accept life with grace and delights. You better remind yourself that you are not done with me. You have reason and cause to be alive. I happen to need you. That is reason enough!"

"Sweet woman, while we are on that wave, as you call it, you do understand that I am losing hope, and you do know what that means. When I am alone, I think of my own reasons for being. You have to admit, there aren't too many reasons. At this time in my life, I can't give much meaning to my existence. I am a man put on earth to serve others. I'm not doing much of that these days. As for you, I know you well enough to recognize that a singular person needs no one. You are capable of handling your own life without me in it. I know you will miss me, and I will hang around as long as I can, and I will tell you when my time is approaching. I spent a fair amount of time attempting to make sense of my own truth. I know it won't be long for my soul's journey to end. This is something I can assure you of.

"Evie, if you can, remember that our journey together will continue because I believe it began eons ago. I do not claim to know what happens on the other side of life, as we know it, but given the opportunity, I will bring you flowers. You will know I am sure of it. How is that?"

"Don, I do not care about what you are saying now. The fact is, I need you to be around me. I finally understand what love is. I know that my discovery is not enough to change the course of our lives. I am selfish. You give me a kind of strength I cannot explain. There is something profound there and I need it. Besides all this, when my back hurts, who will know where to put their hands to restore nerves and push bones into the right places? I told you, I am selfish!"

"Evie, after a great deal of self-examination and contemplation, I have come to believe that my terrestrial consciousness will continue in another form. I feel the soul's journey continues and you and I will find the means to communicate. Trust is what we both need."

Though I did not like the subject of the conversation, we became somewhat comfortable with the explorations. They took place almost every day, and from them, I experienced from anger to pain, laughter to tears.

"Eveline, you must prepare your entire being because we are a good pair. I know it could be more difficult than we think. Neither one of us had died before and remembered it. I have a feeling, when you were writing about my birth, you were also writing about my death. Not mine only, but every birth, and every death."

"Don, I am not an advanced soul. I think you are going way over the threshold of my understanding."

"No, Evie, I'm going exactly where you are. I know you well enough to know that after a while you will get your balance. It is the stuff you're made of."

"So, while all this is happening where are the hands on that clock?"

"Probably 9:45, unless I check out at 10:45. Regardless of ending time, I know that I am close. I am certain of it!

"Eveline, before the end, I have a lot more to tell you. So forget the clock. The hands of time and of growth are not controlled by either of us."

"Don you are so right. All this could be teaching us about acceptance over the things we cannot change. The whole thing sucks! When I divorced the father of my children, I had no remorse, no regrets. The pain was for what it might have been yet never was. This is not the case here!"

Divorce Changes People

"Evie, you got me thinking of the aftermath of my divorce. I know it is different for each person. I used to think the one asking for the divorce recuperated faster. In some cases I am sure it is the case. I have come to understand that only the person without a conscience recovers fast.

"For me, having an addictive personality did not help. Now I see why the marriage could not have worked. There were too many fragments we did not know how to put together. We were not suited for each other. I can tell you, those are not easy facts to accept."

"I see your point Don, since I was the sole supporter of my children. I was concerned only with being mother, father, provider, disciplinarian, cook and a multitude of other things. I had to balance these tasks and emotions with a degree of fun. For sure divorce was not easy for me. It was devastating to have had a husband emotionally so removed from his children that he never made any attempt at being part of their lives. Sometimes I wondered how he coped with himself. But that is not for me to know. The fact is, I think each person copes according to their emotional development and how they face it."

"Evie, if I understand the dynamic, I'd say your marriage started with emotional distance, and soon the abandonment—even if he came home. He was an absentee father and husband. I believe his capacity for such emotions had not settled into who he was. I also speculate that your divorce opened a wide door for you to go through and grow. The person you are today, I like very much, and that is good enough for me."

"I am glad that I had a fairly easy relation with my ex-wife. I attempted to make it less painful for the kids, but I don't know that I ever succeeded. I took the kids on as many vacations as I could manage. When not vacationing, I had a small house in the mountains of northern Arizona. I spent lots of weekends there with my kids. The tremendous difficulty was to bring them back to their mother. Each time a part of my flesh felt as if it was being shredded. When not with the kids, I worked almost non-stop. That was the way I coped. People figured I was a successful businessman. I was the owner of fifty homes, of three real estate companies, and earned some awards of achievement. The assets owned, and I don't know what else, gave me a millionaire's title. Evie, I can tell you all material possessions in the world were not sufficient to fill the inescapable void in my life. I had to face how desperate and unhappy I was. There was cancelled feeling, I had a trove filled with material possessions. Nothing that I possessed occupied the empty space between heart and head.

"I felt isolated, but I did not know from what. There was no one to talk to, and no reason to live another day. In a way, for different reasons, these days I sometimes approach that type of feeling. I am not desperate. I have you to talk to, and that makes the difference in the place where I find myself. But my reason to be alive is like a thin thread. I can see it."

When such conversations took place, as I saw it, we each had a distinct feeling that we were brought together for reasons we did not fully understand. We were encountering feelings neither of us could name or identify.

"Evie, today, as I talk to you about all this, I think of the woman I talked to you about before. She was one of my real estate agents. I think in her own way she loved me dearly. One day, when almost everyone was gone, she came to my office, sat down, looked at me straight in the eyes, leaned forward across the desk, and asked me to look at myself, and find out why I felt so devastated. Then she asked me, was the emptiness because my wife was granted a divorce or was it because I had lost control of what I thought was mine to take for granted. After she spoke her words, she got up and left.

"She was a good person. I did not like losing what for years I had taken for granted to be mine. Evie, I did not like what she said. I did not like her arrogance. I decided I would fire her. After making the decision, I did not feel any better. I could still hear her voice asking me about what I thought was mine. I cried that night!

"It was not easy to admit to myself that I was responsible for my life. Being responsible was a lot more than buying cars and paying for the needs of my family. I think most of us confuse what being responsible means. It's so much easier to point a finger and make others responsible for our wellbeing. What is odd, I was taking care financially of mother, sister, wife, kids, but I didn't know how to be responsible toward them or to myself. I never asked my children how they felt about themselves. I played a role but did not know the script. I continuously hear you with your kids. What an intimate relationship you have. I wish I was more like that with my kids, but it's too late now. They are all adults. But, Evie, I can tell you I like the man I have become. I can't change the past, but I can look at myself and feel responsible for my wellbeing. My soul likes that."

Eveline Horelle Dailey

How AA Changed My Life

"Eveline, I must tell you about my first AA meeting. Gosh, I have been telling you about how I put my shoes on. I might as well talk about AA.

"I went to a meeting because a good friend suggested it. In my utter denial about my drinking problem, I felt the man was crazy. He even followed me as I drove to the address.

"I found a parking spot far from the entrance. I looked around—I had to make sure people who knew me could not have identified my car. There was not one Cadillac in the parking lot—my latest one was five days old.

"It took all the courage I had to open the door and go in. My friend was right behind me. Once inside, I noticed, not one person was wearing a suit. I can tell you my first impression was one of disgust. To me these people were all losers. I, on the other hand, was a successful businessman, with friends in every bar in town.

"I found two empty chairs, way in the back row. My friend found two empty chairs, way in the front. He guided me to the front. I used the word guide loosely. He shoved me. A man walked toward a podium, and for three minutes he talked about losing his home, his job and his family. I had lost none of the things he described. My wife had divorced me, but my family was intact. I could travel where I wanted. I wore a gold watch. I changed cars more often than anyone I knew. This man and I had nothing in common.

"After two or three people talked, I realized the stories were about DUIs, and other problems *they* had. *They* were all grateful since *they* were no longer drinking.

"At one point, I started getting up to leave. My friend grabbed my sleeve and told me to sit down. 'Sit, say nothing, do nothing, and just listen.' After the meeting the entire group stood and recited the Lord's Prayer. I knew it. They also recited the Serenity prayer.

"When I got home, I gave a great deal of thought to that Serenity prayer. To accept the things I could not change—that part hit me like a ton of bricks. A new phrase had been added to my vocabulary. *Alcoholic.* I had to admit to myself that I was one of those losers. I was an alcoholic.

"Sweetheart, I think only an alcoholic can relate to this. To admit that you are an alcoholic is nearly an impossible admission. I had to realize my beliefs about myself were trash. That was unfathomable. To know that I could control people and things and find out I couldn't control myself was heart-wrenching. Most of all, I felt shame, hate, and despair. At one point, while I was vomiting in the bathroom, like a gust of wind coming out of my lungs, I heard: *You are the loser, Dailey*! Eveline, if you ever see one of my children or grandchildren abusing alcohol, please try to intervene. Talk to them. Gently Evie please, not as the bulldozer you become when you talk to your kids. My children would not know what to do with that."

"Wow, Don, you are right. I have no way to understand this. I can only sympathize."

"Now that this illness does not control my life, I know it is a grave ailment. It attacked my head, soul, family and everything I touched. I can't laugh about it because statistically, too many never recover. This experience also showed me how to deal with what is going on in my life now.

"I had to change friends, behavior, where I went, and what thoughts I had. To concentrate on recovering from drunk to sober was imperative to my success. You know Evie, transition does not happen overnight. One day, in that same bathroom, not vomiting, but looking at myself, I realized, I liked being sober. The rest is history."

"I am glad I met you after you became sober. I know I would not have anything to do with a drunk."

"Ha Evie! We do many things to ourselves, but in reality, there are no wrongs. They are part of a road we must walk in order to find equilibrium farther down that road. I learned to reflect, and I learned to look at myself in a mirror. I was popular in Phoenix, Arizona.

"Some new friends felt I should run for office. They took me to the Governor's mansion to meet some people. Soon I realized I did not belong with any of them. They were politicians willing to sell principles for a position in government. Everybody wanted to be powerful. I had found my power.

"I was becoming a person I liked. My power was not coming from people around me. In the mirror I saw promises. By the way, for me, it was one of the many discoveries of sobriety. I was no longer at the effect of alcohol and what people thought about me."

"I am glad you took that giant leap and arrived where you are today. I like and love the person you are Don Dailey!"

"Yes, me too. I like and love the person I am today. I became *better and better than I was before*. I am proud of who I am today. The changes I made in my life allowed my love of learning to return. Even today, as old as I am, I like to explore things I know nothing about. By the way, that's how you know you are alive."

"Donaldo, you are one amazing man! One I admire a bit more every day."

"Evie, you are pretty remarkable, too. I can't count the things I admire about you. I am a proud man! I am sorry I am putting you through so many troubles and heartaches. I know being a caretaker is not like going to a ballgame. Don't laugh; I know you've never been to a ballgame. Just continue to dance around the house as you always do. I like that better, and I like your laughter. Those things you do as you say: *Comme Marie la Folle*, these things bring me life. What does that mean anyway?"

"That means. *Like Marie, the crazy one.*"

"But that makes no sense. Who was Marie?"

"I have no idea. This is something I heard when I was a kid. Especially when I was being silly. So I guess Marie must have been a crazy and silly person. I do not know."

"I recall my sister Catherine telling you that I collected girlfriends. Most were too young for me. She didn't like my arm candy of choice. It became funny when my sister Irene jokingly said that I went to the high school proms to pick up girls. While Catherine thought you would get upset, Irene was delighted to hear you laugh with zest. You made points with my sisters that day."

"What they did not know is when I met you, I had arrived at a place of peace and harmony in my life. What other people did or thought about was no longer my concern.

"I am glad I met you when I did."

"I still laugh about the day you met my entire family. It was a Thanksgiving celebration. Family plus half the people in this state were there. My sister always had tons of people at her house. My nephew once asked me if all those people were relatives. We had a good laugh because we did not know half the people that were there. That reminds me, when I called my sisters to tell her I was bringing you, and you were a vegetarian, she had no reaction. It was hysterical when we got there and I saw her open a can of string beans and a can of corn. What a dinner you had! What a sport you were. I knew you didn't eat canned foods.

"Sweetheart, you are so well polished, but the look on your face that day, told me you were about to die. It was nice of you to thank her for her trouble. Evie, You still melt my heart. You are special to me, and perhaps to my family too."

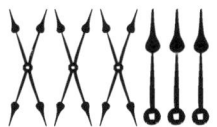

A Monastic Life

"Evie, I like how you told the story of my beginning. Why don't you write something about the time I spent in New Mexico? I told you about that at least a hundred times. You also need to write something about the gun."

"All right Don. I will make a deal with you. When I write, you sleep. When you get up, I will read what I wrote. If you feel up to it, later on, we will go for a short walk. How would that be for you? But first I need to know more details like why you spent time in New Mexico? I know there was a lot happening behind the scene."

"Well, Evie, that is simple. As a human being, I always felt emptiness. The religions that I explored did not fill the empty tank. The new cars that I bought did not bring me comfort, either. I know friends told you I changed cars all the time. Not true. I never changed a Cadillac before the tires wore out. I wanted something, but I didn't know what it was. I also didn't know where to find it. Pretty much the way you say your life works, *things happen*. I met a monk and soon after another. Their sense of peace had an impact on me."

"A monk! Where in heaven's name does one meet a monk? Did you go to Tibet or Nepal or some other such place? You did not tell me about that part."

"No, I met a monk, an American Monk, from Spencer Abbey. He was dressed in civilian clothes. I was at a restaurant about to have dinner. I was alone. He had begun his meal, and for some reason talked to me from across the aisle. A while later, he asked if he could join me. He was not used to eating alone, and I normally had a girlfriend with me. I said yes.

"He thanked me, moved his stuff and sat opposite. He told me, it was a rare occasion to eat in a place where he could talk. Allowing him to join me was a gift. At first I thought he was weird, then he continued. He told me he was a monk. I think I went into a state of shock. In his abbey, in New Mexico, they did not talk while eating. I had never given such ideas or discipline a second of my time. Besides, I talk all day long. At one point he said something that literally went through me!"

"And what was that?"

"He said he was back visiting the world that he had left behind. He was going to give some blood at a clinic. He said during this short time in Phoenix, he enjoyed talking to some people, like myself. After a few days in Arizona, he was going to Boston to visit his family. When I asked him why he became a monk, he explained that for years he was a businessman in Boston. He had successes, but he felt he was empty. He felt he needed to change something in his life. It was not a vacation he needed, but a break from everything he knew.

"Evie, for once in my life, I had no words.

"He said he needed a new discipline. He had lost his sense of ideals, and the reality of *here and now* was missing in his life. He said he was tired of settling, and had no sense of what was real and important in his life. He had made money, had met with some interesting challenges—women too, he said. But most of all, there was no gentleness in his life.

"Evie, the more he spoke, the more something resonated inside of me. He had been at the monastery for five years. He went on to tell me, once he arrived in New Mexico at the abbey it took only a few days for something to change within him. For the first time he understood freedom, yet he could not go anywhere.

"He gave me a moment to think. He took a few bites and went on to explain life at the monastery. He explained that he found the freedom to meet his own spirit. Those Evie, were perhaps the most compelling words I had heard in a long time. He was able to grow something inside of him that he knew was there all along. He didn't know how to extract it from within.

"I was dumbfounded. He had taken this vacation because his twin brother was dying, and he wanted to spend some quality time with him. This man did not try to convince me of anything. He did not even ask me what I did for a living. Whatever he was saying, I needed to hear."

"Don. I believe this is the way of the cosmos. Things we know nothing about are brought to us. We can experience them or reject them. I have done both."

"The waitress brought my food. He ate with a kind of appreciation on his face. He seemed utterly pleased with his meal or himself. I couldn't determine which.

"After we finished our meal, he suggested that perhaps I would enjoy a moment at Spencer Abbey. He felt I would gain something from it. On a napkin, he gave me the address. He made up a map I could follow to get there. I noticed that the monastery was past Abiquiu, where the artist Georgia O'Keefe resided, but not by much. I had seen one painting of O' Keefe and I liked it. I figured I could go visit her studio, maybe meet her. I would visit the Monastery afterwards. They were just northeast of her place.

"Was this monk sent to meet my spirit? I don't know. It felt strange. He told me his order was the Cistercians; they are a Roman Catholic religious order. Aside from the fact that they wore a robe and a cassock, he told me about the major endeavors which consisted of academic pursuits. I liked that idea. They also observed a life of self-sufficiency. We exchanged a few more words and we parted company. I kept the napkin.

"Later on I learned that this order began in France in 1098 from what the Benedictines order had become. I am sure you have heard about them or St. Benedict.

"Evie, I'm tired. I could stand the fresh air you suggested. You think you could push me around the lake? I would enjoy that. I love the scenery, but I don't think I could walk this afternoon. I enjoy that place, and every time I see a duck, I think of you and the first book you wrote. *Lessons from the Lakeside*. Moma the duck is all over that lake."

"Donaldo, you have a deal. I too enjoy that lake, and who knows, we may meet St. Francis feeding the birds."

"Hey sweetheart, remember the light of God surrounds you. The Power of God protects you. Wherever you are, God is. When you write about this, just let it flow. You have a good pen."

It was many years before we met that Don decided he needed to explore his spirituality. He had studied a few religions and learned something from each. None offered him what was lacking inside. Decades before, he had parted company with the Catholic Church. He knew the comfort level he was seeking was within the teachings of a Christian denomination. Since he had been an altar boy, he explained to me he already knew rigidity. He knew the prayers, and he knew the songs he could not sing.

I suppose when a child is born of extreme poverty and he does not differentiate tones, there are no means to find out the reason for that. He also had one eye that was lazy and slowly it stopped seeing much. He compensated for the ninety percent loss of vision with his good eye.

He was lucky when he went into the Air Force. The vision test was self-administered because the young soldier testing him was preoccupied with a beautiful girl.

Each time he spoke to me about his New Mexico experience, he made sure I understood he had a need: exploration of a deeper part within himself. He did not know what it was, but it was something he needed to do. He also told me he met many people with philosophies similar to the monk he had met.

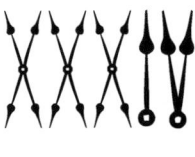

A Gun

"Evie, when I first told you about these things, you only listened. I told you I shot myself. You did not seem to judge me. You looked puzzled, but did not ask why. You respected my privacy until I was ready to share more. You did not seem shocked by either story.

"You know sometimes, you puzzle the heck out of me. I am going to tell you about the gun. Do you have time to listen?"

"Don, of course, I have time. Do you want to tell me now, here sitting by the table, or do you want to go to the lake?"

"Lets do it here. It's a short story. We can go to the lake after. If you are not tired that is!

"By the way, I think on the clock this sort of thing happens about past the halfway mark. A lot of life has been experienced, but there is only emptiness.

"I have to tell you, when somebody has no particular interest in guns, it takes a while to put a bullet into the barrel. I hate to admit it. I had a hard time figuring out how to do this. In the navy, I never used a gun. In the Navy I learned how to use binoculars.

"When I got the gun from a friend, I did not even look at it. I think he assumed I knew about guns. He needed some money, and I had some. Of course, by now you know I am not mechanically inclined. To me this was all about mechanics. Putting a bullet into the gun was a lot harder than in the cowboy movies. Eventually, I figured it out. I looked at that gun for at least twenty minutes. I thought of my entire family. In my own mind, I wished them all well and said farewell. No one knew what I was about to do. No one cared.

"I kept looking at the hole where the bullet would come out—the barrel held me hostage. Time went by. Evie, it was not so easy to take my life. I called each of my children. They had no idea how desperate I was. It occurred to me, I never learned to communicate with my family. I talked a lot, but I could never explain to them how I felt.

"I talked to my kids, my sisters, and they were all well. I told them I loved them—I always did. Six times, I hung up. I don't know how long I looked into the barrel. I went into a kind of meditation. I kept saying *I love you* to myself. I think it did not register. We say that thousands of times, but often they are just words. Thinking about the kids, I realized, that time, when I told them that I loved them, it had a meaning like it never had before."

"Don, I cannot fathom the agony of desperation. I have used these words too many times without a thought."

"Evie, you know, the sadness of it all is that I don't know how to talk to my kids. We talk, but we really don't say anything. Listening to you and your children, the laughter and the tears, and the bonding is something I missed out on. I am learning. Thank you, sweetheart. I am learning.

"I must say, sometimes when I hear you talk to your kids, I want to laugh, and sometimes you scare me. I am forever thinking *they'll never talk to her again.* Two minutes later I hear your laugh on the phone. It is music to my ears. I don't know that I will get there with my kids. I am only learning. You talk to them from your gut and I guess they do the same because I've heard you cry on the phone. It's the laughter that gets me each time. I love it.

"I hope my kids realize how much I love them. I can tell you, I was a father who gave all the material things they wanted or needed. I now know it takes a lot more to be a father. I know, as a parent, I failed them many times. I am not proud of that."

"Don, it takes a great man, a man of courage, to utter such words. I think you are wrong. Your kids know how much you adore them. I can tell you all parents make mistakes. We do not know how to raise children. It is rather backward; we are too young when we have them. That is, however, the way nature decided it would be. Almost anyone can have a child. That has to do with the law governing the joining of sperm and egg. Parenting is a whole different thing. We carry with us the illusion that we will be better parents than our own. No one tells us how. We rely on immature instincts, religions, schools, and so on. Unfortunately, most of us do not have a clue about the enormity of what being a parent is. I think if people knew, we would not live in an overpopulated world."

"Yes, I guess I was trying to do something about overpopulation."

"Don, you are getting as sarcastic as me."

"Now back to my gun story. I am not sure when I pulled the trigger. I was sitting at my desk. I missed my heart. I can tell you the physical pain was not something I ever anticipated. I was supposed to be dead. What scared me most was my blood all over the place. New carpeting installed in my office a couple of weeks before had blood all over it."

"You are funny. You attempted suicide. It did not work, and you were concerned about blood on carpet. You are funny alright."

"Something clicked inside of me. I became instantly more aware of *me*. The real me, Evie. I called a friend to have the carpet cleaned, and then I called the police. I was in control. I handled the things I needed to do immediately. In an instant, I knew there was a change in me. Suddenly I had purpose. My life became clear to me.

"I was stunned because I was supposed to be dead. I was also in a state of grace because I knew something had changed in me. Evie, I may never be able to express all the feelings. It was one of awareness, a knowing. I was alive, but in a different way. I can't explain it."

"Don, I am finding this fascinating. Perhaps because it did not happen on my watch, so kindly, tell me more."

"I am convinced that a part of me did die. I immediately felt and still do that my soul had gone through some kind of transformation. I don't know how to explain it. Maybe this is when I found who I was. Only one person talked to me about this feeling. All I can tell you is that I felt my soul did some kind of an exchange. I don't know the words to explain what I felt. You saw my Lobsan Rampa books, and you had them too, so I know you understand what I am saying.

"It was after this incident that I began to explore many spiritual avenues. I spoke to many people possessing a lot of wisdom. I wanted to find out what had happened to me. I joined churches and spiritual groups. It was at the monastery that I found the tools of understanding, but that is for later.

"You know, Evie, in life, many of us are taught never to talk about certain things. My immediate family knows about this attempt. Most people including extended family or grandchildren do not know, at least I don't think they know. Telling you this, I am thinking about my mother who said thousands of times, "there are things we don't talk about." She was wrong. Today, here I am talking about it. The gun became an instrument to bring me to an *opening* to a new self. I am eternally grateful for that."

"You know Don, when I told you we were culturally different, I did not realize how much. I can only think that if a member of my family attempted suicide, I believe they would talk about it for a long time. Understanding why would have been a motivator. Only after understanding, support would perhaps have followed."

"Evie, when I briefly told you about the gun, the time was not right to talk more. I had just met you, and talking extensively about it would not have been appropriate. Friends and family never said a word about Don Dailey shooting himself. There is shame to such things. Religion says you can't take your own life. I am here to tell that you can. We confuse our flesh with what life is.

Family and two friends came to visit me at the hospital. No one else knew that I had voluntarily shot myself. Not one person ever asked me why. Eveline, I think this is the way families carry self-imposed shame for generations. I guess I am to blame because I didn't talk about it either. I am glad we are talking about it now.

"I had to clarify for myself if I felt shame and or guilt about this. The thing is, decades had passed and whatever the feelings I may have had were no longer any part of my life. But now I know well it was something that had to happen for me to become who I am today. I now have neither shame nor guilt. I have understanding. It was an episode of my life, a chapter I had to go through in order to venture in a different direction. Amazing how things work.

"I am glad that there is understanding between us. We both know it is not easy to divulge the things we did that society finds something wrong with. It's so easy to judge what's wrong or what's right without knowing any of the whys. The relationship we have with our psychology does not seem to enter our conscious mind until much later. We did good Evie, we survived!"

"Yes, Donaldo. I am glad for that. We have discussed many times the psychological reasons why in moments of fear we all do things that we normally would not. People also judge others because they are influenced by where they are in their development in life. I have learned in my life that I cannot judge people or even what I have done. There are always reasons, and at the end of all speculations, there are lessons that need to be learned. As you have said many times, it is all part of a soul's journey. Predestined, if I may."

"Evie, today I like the idea that in any situation I know, there are no mistakes."

"Gosh Donaldo, I do love you more than you will ever know."

"Yes, you are right. All that happened in my life showed me what gratitude was all about. It took a gunshot to propel me to study many things. Getting a few degrees amounts to only a paper at the end of a junction on a road. Learning about the mind in general, and learning about many great minds, I have been able to help some people with theirs. I am proud of that. My greater accomplishment was that I stopped drinking! So what do you say now that you have all the details?"

"Don, like your friend told you, I have a feeling what you felt was your soul transferring hosts. Maybe the one you were born with had to go. I am glad that the man I met, with the same or a different soul, is the man I married. I think some call such exchanges something like a *drop-in*. You mentioned Rampa. I remember through one of his books he explained his own similar circumstances. There are many mysteries to be accepted, and not questioned.

"Don, I like your soul just the way it is. I am grateful for who you are in my life. I gather the other soul was not too happy where it was. I cannot expand further on any of it because I know little about such things. I am glad you told me. Now when they take X-rays of your chest, I can explain the pieces of lead they do not ask about."

"Evie, I remember smiling a lot when before our marriage we were going through our books. Once I saw *The Third Eye, The Hermit, The Doctor from Lhasa*, and the others, I knew you and I would be just fine. Looking at the state of wear in the Rampa books, I knew we each read them more than once. It felt good to know that our interests traversed worlds. What got you interested in this mystic from Tibet?"

"I think it must have been a hundred years ago. I heard one man tell a story. I no longer remember the story, but it was one that caught my attention. I wrote the name and decided to check out this Rampa author. I purchased the collection after reading the first book.

"Don, as you talked of your suicide attempt, the idea of a soul transfer of course came to mind. After all, souls are said to be eternal, and sometimes they may need a body to carry on. As I know you today, I can see the possibility. There is something that elevates my own soul when I think of such likelihood. I know the work you have done. I know the work you continue to do. Your life expresses that you are not an ordinary Joe. I enjoy that you do not qualify what you do as work, or a calling, you just do it! I am honored to be part of your life. I know you are not at all an ordinary man."

We continued our conversation, as always jumping subjects like the crickets we once encountered long ago when we began our walk together. In both our cases we chose to explore the gifts in our individual lives.

"You know, Evie, not one doctor ever asked me about shrapnel inside my chest. X-ray technicians, because of my age, probably figured I got those in Korea. No one ever asked. Each time no one asks, my mother comes to me. 'Donnie, people don't ask such questions.' I think people do not talk about these things because they are afraid to know about them. This could be because more people than not have given thought to ending their lives. Perhaps they do not want to be reminded."

It was a good four hours later that we came back to the monastic life. There is something remarkable about a man who does not shy away from his truth. I liked that about him. What a gift this man was in my life and that of many others.

For reasons I cannot explain, time and place rarely hold great importance to me. It was not any different during these conversations.

Today, I regret not asking about the timetable in his imaginary clock. I would venture to say it was a time of awakening.

Spencer Abbey

"Thank you, Evie. I enjoy it when you take me around the lake. I know how difficult it is to get that wheelchair in and out of the car. I am not very much help, am I? I also worry about your back."

"Don, most people do not have, in a lifetime, the help you give me in one day. You give me emotional support. You nourish my inspirations to continue to write, to paint or to weave. You encourage me to be all that I am. You are like my parachute, and because of you, I can fly! If you were not able to take a step on your own, that would perhaps be different. I could not lift you. We are fine just the way things are. We are able to exercise gratitude and meaningful conversations—That too, few couples can honestly have. I know how tired you get with the walker around the lake. A pair of lungs is something we all take for granted. The wheelchair is a godsend. I must admit, some of the doctors are good for something. One of them prescribed it."

"Evie, all this fresh air has made me hungry."

"No problem. Before we went out, I put the vegetable soup out. We are going to have a bowl, and after that, I have a brand new Tiramisu and coffee for desert. I even have the crackers you like with your soup."

"You think of everything. I admire this about you. Somehow no matter what goes on with me, you find a way to be focused on what you need to do. Did you put enough salt into the soup? I need to taste something."

"Yes sir, I did. I gave up thinking that a little salt would hurt you. I know you and everyone else needs some salt. I read that garlic enhances taste buds, so I added some too!"

"I like the way you put a lot of potatoes into the vegetable soup. My Irish roots are pleased. I will be happy to have a large bowl when we get home.

"Evie, as I told you, the search for finding my spiritual self became very important. Even now, with my sedentary life, I discover something new every day. Years ago, I physically healed from the gunshot; I was not restored to wholeness. Medical establishments are not concerned about people's wholeness. I think they have no idea that a body contains many parts. The most important parts can't be seen with the eyes. So when the body is affected by something it doesn't know the spirit and the soul are influenced also.

"To continue the monastery saga, let me tell you more. One day, coming out of a meeting, a man stopped me. He said he was sitting behind me, and felt it was all right to talk to me. Evie, you know I talked to everyone, so this was just one more stranger in need of somebody to talk to. I was on my way home to watch TV and make myself a Cornish game hen. I knew how to cook those and I liked them. Actually, I was an expert. I also had a box of macaroni and cheese. The man kept on talking. Since I had two hens, I invited this man to come over for dinner. I had never seen him before. Yet I felt compelled to invite him over. I questioned my sanity.

"He was from Pennsylvania. I enjoyed dinner with him, and conversation too. This guy did not look hungry. There was, however, an aura about him, something I can't explain. He was bright. Your friend John Henry Waddell, the sculptor, has that same brightness. When I met

John, it was the first time I was seeing that in another person. You have a few friends with that nameless brightness.

"Once inside my place I went to the kitchen, and he went straight to a pile of books I was reading. He sat by the dining table and looked though the books. He somehow became aware that I was looking for some type of spiritual guidance. The books he looked at covered a variety of philosophies. As I prepared the birds, he began to talk about his own spirituality. He said he was happy that his wrong turn took him to meet me.

"He seemed interested in everything around the living room. He asked me if I had read all the books he saw. He asked me if I had found what I was looking for. I told him, I had not found what I was looking for, but that I was venturing in new thoughts. He opened up. He told me he was in Phoenix for a short time, but he did not tell me why he was here. Then he said he had to return to the Abbey where he resided. He told me he was a monk and his name was Peter. I nearly dropped the macaroni and cheese. In less than a month I had met two monks. What a coincidence! I am not sure coincidence was the word to use but, it was the only one I had. I felt there was more to these encounters.

"He talked a great deal about the order. He was a monk and New Mexico was home, though he was born in Pennsylvania. Evie, the man talked more than I do. This was the second time I was meeting a monk from New Mexico. I didn't know there were monasteries there. When I asked him if he was an alcoholic, he said no. He explained at length, it was his first time in Phoenix, and he was lost. He could not find any public place to ask for directions. He then saw lots of cars entering the parking lot. He followed, figuring he would find someone able to give him directions.

"According to the monk, people were going through a set of double doors, and one of them suggested that he too should go in. Everyone seemed friendly, so he entered this hall. A man selling tickets for something showed him where there were single seats. Mine was the seat in front of him."

"Don, the universe has a grandiose way of taking care of you. Was this man the head monk?"

"There are monks, priests, and some abbots. I had no idea what his rank was. It didn't matter to me. He had an inner worldly peace. As he spoke, I noticed something particularly peaceful about him. Evie, I have been speaking so much, I am hungry again. May I have another piece of that Tiramisu? I enjoyed the taste of it! Would you believe, I tasted it. Give me a bigger piece this time."

There is a good feeling when a patient is eating anything. As a caretaker, that spelled success to me. The only problem was, my patient enjoyed what was either too sweet or too salty.

"Do you want a glass of milk with it?"

"No. I have some coffee left."

I got him a piece of Tiramisu, and half a glass of almond milk. He looked at me smiling. When I faced him, he had a way of raising himself from his sitting position and put both his hands on my shoulders, his thumbs, resting on my collarbones, almost touching each other. His other fingers gave my back a quick massage. Those were moments of endearment I enjoyed a great deal. Each time, I also receive a kiss to open my third eye. Practicing Yoga, and also being a Buddhist, I understood that various parts of my body are energy centers. It was also a sort of a benediction. To complete the blessing, we locked gaze.

"The light of God surrounds you." Don said.

I responded with: 'The power of God protects you." It was a litany he recited often. I never knew the rest of the prayer, but it was one that was important to him.

In our lives, there were rituals, and only we were invited. It felt good to be the recipient of this type of light.

"After talking to two monks, and reading a great deal about the monastic way of life, my intention was to become a man of the cloth. That took me to a monastery in New Mexico, Spencer Abbey, on a hill north of Abiquiu. It was the place both men had spoken of. By the way, after we ate, this well-spoken monk, in regular clothes, thanked me. He got into his rental car and left. I never saw him again.

"I drove about fourteen hours. I stopped many times to measure what was going on inside. I was silently asking myself if I really wanted to do this. Every place I rested I enjoyed the magic of New Mexico. Following my map, I eventually made the turn. A hundred feet down the road a lush forest welcomed me. I stopped the car. The heavy wooded area gave me the solitude I needed to think one more time. In no time, I was sure this place held something for me. I went there with the intention of entering a different way of life.

"The recent dramatic event in my life shaped within me a need for clarity. I was not sure I knew what clarity looked like. I don't know how long I was there. The Cadillac was idling. The heat was on. After a while I drove toward the front door, parked my car, and walked the cold hallways. There was no one to greet me, but I did not turn back. I walked a few more feet, and noticed a light coming from an opening to a room. I went in. There was a long table to the side, a few chairs, and lots of books were on the table. No one was there. This made no sense to me, yet something inside me felt reinforced. I had a sense of being awakened. A monk came out of a room and invited me in. A new life began to unfold."

"Donaldo, what an incredible restoration of who you were all along! Your life is the stuff fiction is made of. If I tell all the stories you told me, no one will ever believe me. Those who know you do not know this side of you. I am sure of it. You do not display who you really are. You do not let people into your world. I am privileged, honored, and grateful."

"In that case let me tell you more. The thing is once I was able to be truthful with myself, what I went there for was accomplished—this is why I didn't become a monk. It took about nine and a half months, and no one knew where I was because once a month, I was in Phoenix and I saw my two children who resided there. No one knew what I was doing. No one ever asked.

"It was during that time, I came to realize I did not need to live my life for the approval of others. Did I ever tell you, during our first walk, I noticed you lived your life without that need for approval? You seemed to be guided, and that was approval enough for you. You had an inner freedom I spent a long time searching for."

"Don, I am glad for the developments in our lives. Who knew one phone call to go for a walk would change both our lives? Odd the way the cosmos works. Who knew?"

"Evie, did I tell you after I left the monastery, I stayed in contact with Father Bernard? He was from Canada. When I told him I was satisfied with what I had learned, and I was going back to Phoenix to stay, he told me that every worthy human endeavor required an ideal. He was glad that I found mine—something else I discovered while there. Once I recognized my weaknesses and struggles, they seemed to just drop off. It was not a matter of effort, as I always believed. I had come to understand that I, and my understanding of God, was part of the same universe. Eventually, I was able to align my body, my mind, and my spirit.

"That day of my departure, Father Bernard gave me a bear hug and sent me on my way. He wished me to stay on the path of my own approval. Those few words meant the world to me. He also said continual learning was excellent. In the end, Evie, the experiences in life lead to wisdom. We have a lifetime to develop the practices we wish to engage ourselves in. I found these things while listening to what Father Bernard had to say. The man was great!"

"What a formidable teacher and friend you found in this man. Imagine each human being encountering such a person. The amount of knowledge absorbed in one sitting could change the world. Do you know how fortunate I am to know you as I do?"

With that experience he told me he made other discoveries. Fancy cars, houses, money, and women left him without the sense of fulfillment he felt he could find outside of himself. He insisted that it was upon this discovery that he became aware of the impermanence of everything including that of the self.

"You know, Evie, once I discovered the things we talked about, I realized I had conquered who I was. I became accepting of myself. I learned to love myself. Up to that point, the successes of my life had left me with a meaningless existence."

"Donaldo, it seems to me that this place was responsible for the advancement of the true you. So what else did you learn there? I need to know."

"Freedom, Evie. I discovered the freedom to be me. The freedom to explore the person I am. That monastery and the monks influenced my personal growth in a way no one had before. Talking there was done only for about an hour a day. In other words, these discoveries came from within me. I have a feeling you understand that. The freedom to find the value of my being, and to be true to it, was the greatest discovery I made there. The lure and serenity of the place, however, was not enough to keep me in."

For a while, he said he travelled life alone, calling his children and sisters as often as he could. When he returned to Phoenix he spent time with them. He did not tell them much about what he was doing. This lack of communication with his children was also a difference between us. He was continuously puzzled by the relationship I had with mine—my children and I were a trio growing and following directions from the cosmos. Our conversations were filled with challenges, laughter, and tears.

"Evie, while at the monastery, I learned to use the mind that had tormented me for most of my life for my own good. After I left, I began to refine who I was becoming—a me that had been lost. I discovered my own path, my own truth. I may never be able to explain how satisfied I am with myself today. I also know I can't ever tell you how glad I am that you are in my life. To share the rest of the journey with you is my reward."

This man brought enigma and smiles to my life. At times, my life was nothing but frustration because I could not achieve the mastery he had.

In my mind, there was room to ponder and assimilate some of the things he was saying. In order to grow a bit more, every day I entered that space of *nothingness*. Thinking about his quest, and having spent time with him, I became aware that he ate the fruits of his discoveries. Today, I smile again as I know Donald Thomas Dailey never saw his own luminescence. I have come to believe our own light often blinds us. This was perhaps the case in his life.

Cognizant of our talents for exploration, we decided we would spend time and energy in further pursuits of what made us who we were—two people experiencing personal freedom to grow.

"Evie, your eyes sparkle. They feed a part of me that is slowly but surely dissipating. You refresh my environment. I especially enjoy the momentary lapse of reality. When I hold your hand, you bring light to my vision, yet I like the space between us. I love all the conversations we decided to have as a condition of our marriage. Too often people do not talk. For us, there is happiness, frustration, laughter, and tears. And we talk! It's a good thing. I am a content man. I do not own you, nor do you own me. I think when two people discover this they are on their way to great adventures. I feel as if I were a man walking in grace."

"Donaldo, I believe no matter what is difficult in our lives, the very *nature* of our relationship advances our world toward grace. No matter how crazy I get, what I do, what I say, how I attempt to escape reality, that grace never leaves. I too feel as you do."

Let's Go For A Short Walk

Remote Viewing

Don was a man who explored many avenues of his psyche. Feeling there was something inviolable about what he had gained, he decided to investigate *Remote Viewing*. I had attempted some astral traveling. I was perhaps, too close to my ego, and that prevented any success. Don's suggestion was a new experience. We were observing our relationship, particularly the direction of its soul's growth. This new idea felt like the natural progression of our adventures together.

We met a teacher who had worked for a space and military exploration agency. Don knew two of his students. I am not even sure that these men were students. I only know they knew about it. It took a small amount of enticement. We decided to explore this mental or psychic faculty normally inaccessible to the five senses.

Ours being a relationship based on intentional exploration of all that we were gave us the permission we needed. This approach to life brought us face-to-face with many teachers.

Into our home, came one such teacher to show us this peculiar form of intuition. This man had worked with Stephan Schwartz, an important face in the world of parapsychology, clairvoyance, intuition. It took a few sessions to understand our own sense of inner trust. That was good. That was very good. Soon enough we also discovered that this was not a path for either of us. Perhaps extrasensory perception would be more to our liking. We, however, did not investigate this avenue.

We had many of these side trips in our marriage, and each time we came out knowing there was one thinker and it was neither of us. The *universal mind* was the concept that resonated with my understanding.

Remote Viewing puzzled us and became one of the side trips *we* took in our marriage. It took practice to understand and learn to use our conscious mind to go outside of consciousness and see what others could not see. We could see from lands to small buildings. We could draw them. We were not thinking, we were viewing, feeling the consciousness of others. Don had incredible experiences. He could see/draw and describe things with accuracy. In my case I was not always accurate.

Without intention for outcomes this exercise became voiceless and without reason. We both concluded endeavoring in this practice was a violation of our concepts of human trust. We felt there was infiltration and intrusion without permission. We decided not to become participant in a practice that would not enhance who we wanted to be. We realized later that Remote Viewing could be used for good.

"Evie, I am glad I experienced the monastic way of being. Now I am sure the exploration of life is a singular process. I am glad you as a singular person are able to listen to your heart and your gut. I think this is what life needs from us. This concept, by the way, brings me to the doors of acceptance of many things."

The principles he talked about became guidelines to live by. I came to believe we were explorers. The roads we travelled, arduous and challenging at times, were cleared of boulders only after examination. I had a vision of us, in Khaki clothes and pith helmets, discovering from mountains to shores. We knew we had the tools to either move boulders, or to go around them. We managed to do our growing singularly. Yet we assisted one another, always.

Along with telling me his stories, he read almost every essay and article I ever wrote. I must admit, there is something prideful about having been a featured writer.

Here, these days, to write this work, there is something glorious when a story contains the scent and the music resembling the subject. This man—head of his tribe—managed to entangle his life with mine. Calling him *patriarch* became my manner of a celebration long overdue. I do not believe he set out to be that, but the road he chose to travel made him so. If I have one prayer, it is that the words he spoke penetrate deep inside others. He was a brilliant teacher. Between the lines spoken or written, he managed to show different perspectives for the same subject. Absorption and digestion were often difficult.

"Evie, at each corner of a life, change awaits us all. For me, once I was able to understand this, everything became a source to grow from. I believe, as we go about our lives, we don't give these things any thought. We are too busy escaping what we don't want to look at. I can tell you, our daily communication while having breakfast is a habit that continuously promotes great comfort to me. In a sense, if we had explored remote viewing beyond, I think we would have enhanced our abilities to see further than our own noses. It was a matter of our consciousness at the time.

"Being able to work from home made you a focused individual. I could never do that. Actually I tried and at every opportunity, I left what I was doing to go chase some rainbow. Early on I learned when you were working, there was no need to talk to you. You know at first, I felt rejected."

"The challenges we bring to this old table are tools for introspective thinking and growth. Don, you have no idea how much I enjoy the time we spent just talking. Thank you."

No Ruler and No Gauge

In order to live fully, we avoided gauging life, which went on despite summation. Life went on. Diseases or aging were not the argument with time or with life.

"Evie, people are not their maladies. You can't identify people by their profession—at least you *should* not. We should, therefore, not identify people by the maladies they have."

He did not refer to himself as a cancer survivor. He was not a victim of congestive heart failure. He was not a congestive obstructive pulmonary disease victim. He was not a victim of Parkinson's. He took on these maladies one after the other, living as full a life as he could. He did it with one kidney. He was a man of grace and an enormous amount of courage.

I believe it takes a person of strength to handle and accept without anger the deadly force lurking behind a door—the angel of death was patient and we knew it. To live fully conscious was a condition to accept life on life's terms. I learn these things conversing with this master. He suggested that if one would observe the movement of the tides the meaning of acceptance would become evident. Water comes and water goes, only the moon controls the flux and the reflux.

He often said, "it is in the *observation* that we get to hear the *messages*." I know he was correct.

He also told me as much as he talked, it was in the silence of his mind that he heard the messages of his heart. We had long discussions about these concepts. He managed to teach me that my body and my soul were not the same. After a while, I began to understand it was unnecessary to ever attempt to convince people of anything, since we were on a different journey. Not a religious man, he believed in a divine power and guidance, as he would say, *to nullify all that was not right for him.*

"That which is in my essence is also the essence of the universe. Evie, it took me a long time, a lot of study and reflection, to understand this idea. I meditated on this simple truth, and somehow I added it to my awareness. With all that I learned, I turned my life around. My attitude about everything changed. To find my center, I had to recondition my subjective mind. Of course we are always at the effect of something. It is in awareness that I brought understanding of my own truth.

"Evie, there is something creative always going on inside. Acceptance of the ultimate creative intelligence—regardless of what we call it—is the source of my personal freedom."

"And you, Mr. Dailey, dare to question why I call you a patriarch? Are you aware that most men or women do not travel the depth of the thoughts you have? Most people do not have the capacity to go where your thinking process takes you.

"Dailey, sometimes you get me real pissed. You do not take yourself seriously enough."

"Evie, I think I do. For example, I learned to listen some of the time. I've also learned to give advice when asked. You listen to me, and think I am telling you things you didn't know? Yet, you are not helpless. I know you are able to contribute to what I say, and to what I am telling you. I feel what I feel, and no one can change this. There is a knowing there. I can't explain it. Not even to myself. So sweetheart, all I can tell you is that every day, I listen a little better. I do take myself seriously."

Sometimes, I was awestruck by few words or by none at all. Determined to experience life as presented to him, he decided to tell me more stories. I learned to listen—listening better, better than before.

"Evie, it seems that in order to learn a thing or two, I had to collect a few diseases. Call it God, the Cosmos, the Universe, and better yet Energy; all I know is that I worked hard to find the content of my soul. Circumstances around consciousness showed me that my body happens to be the vehicle this soul needed. I believe my soul, the new one that dropped in, that *too* is part of my life experience. I don't talk about that. Forget I said that. I haven't figured *its* meaning. Regardless of what people may think, there is one universal soul. I see it as kind of an ocean. I feel it. We are a bunch of droplets that makes up that ocean. My part in it is making both soul and body one unit to benefit those I can. I know I am not crazy, and I know you understand me."

"Yes, I do understand you. Perfectly."

"Evie, the first time you said Namaste to me I had to look it up. Once I found that my soul could salute the soul of another, there was no room to hate or to disregard. Like you, I may disagree with people or things and I still can see them as divine beings. People judge, kill, and bless indiscriminately. I used to accept and rationalize all the reasons why it was so. I no longer can be part of that mindset. It changed when I was not looking.

"One word: *Namaste*. Imagine that, Evie. Saluting the soul of another person even if I do not particularly like him or her.

"I think it is during the many corridors and alleys I walked in and out of, that I came to realize with certainty that I am not my body! I don't like the idea of so many diseases, but that's the way it is. I think most of us forget. We all come with an expiration date. The diseases are ganging up on me, but while I am alive, I must live! Prepare yourself. I will tell you the stories I can't write any more. I will show you how to discover the rest."

"Donald. I am ready. I finished the new book and now I am all yours—completely devoted to you. No more escape. The more I hear the stories you have been telling me, the more I know and admire the remarkable person that I will miss."

"Evie, I feel because we talk about matters of life and death with openness, I have become more accepting of the process. I am also more aware of my life, and how I must be true to myself regarding the end of my life. Because we talk so much, I am a better person. Your essence also inspires. "

"I am glad you used the title that was given to you. *The Drum Made from the Skin of My Sisters* is powerful, but after reading the book, I believe it is the best title you could have given to the stories of the two girls. You talk of my courage—the girls you introduce to us knew courage, firsthand."

"Don, you are so kind, biased too. Would you have read this book if it was not written by me?"

"Evie, this is a loaded question. My frame of reference about women's issues is minimal, at best. If I had not met you, I would only know what I am told on TV about women of the Middle East. Come to think of it, I would not know anything at all about people from that region of the world. Remember I have not been exposed to women from other societies. I have not been exposed to men of other societies either. Based on what I just said, I would not have picked up the book. If, however, I read the back of the book, or a random passage, I would have gotten it. Once I read the book, I became aware of my part in minimizing women. For instance, I loved my first wife, but I saw her as my property. I didn't physically abuse her consequently the scars she carried no one saw. I was raised not to physically hurt women, but it took your book to bring me a fresh look at abuse. The men in your book were not groomed to respect girls and women. Their cultures made it so, as did mine.

"Evie, I am sure you know, here, we tend to see people from other places, with cultures different from ours as *less* than whatever *we* think we are. I see your book as one with educational value. I wish I was in a position to make sure that people would learn something from it."

"You are hired. I need a PR person!"

"What bothers me these days about myself is that I can't type anymore. Parkinson's is not easy to deal with. When I look at my hands, I don't see any tremors, yet I can tell when I am using my-smarter-than-I-am phone, I can't hit the letters I want. And the computer is no better. My fingers do not strike in the direction that my head wants. I am also aware of losing control of other movements. Sometimes I wonder what is worse, my breathing or using my hands?

"Evie, do you know how proud I am of you? Deciding to take on your most recent book project showed me one more time how focused you are when you make up your mind. I know those who sent you threatening emails did not scare you. Many people here, and in the Middle East, will not like your book. Those able to think for themselves will find its merit. Most men could learn something from it."

"You are a kind man, Donaldo."

"Evie, now that you agreed to help me, I would like to tell you only funny stories, but unfortunately, life is not all about fun. I know you will have a hard time if you ever decide to take on the project of writing a book on my behalf. I lose chronology. I tell stories. It's not a matter of losing my mind, at least not completely, but dates and times no longer hold the importance they once held. I now know how time and dates have very little control over one's life.

"By the way, Evie, you know what we consider secrets are never as powerful as we think. It's what we keep ruminating on that takes over our lives. Once we tell the people involved about the secrets we have, they no longer have control over us. I must admit, these days, it's all about losing control—the control of my freedom of movement. I can tell you, and no one else, I don't like that at all. Not driving, even if I have one heck of a driver, is perhaps the hardest thing to resolve. It never occurred to me that one day, in my life, I would not be able to drive.

"As I become less engaged in this matter of being alive, I also realize, when events happen, it's not that imperative to know what time it is, or what time is left on my clock. In my case, I know the clock is running out of time. I also know it's how I react to anything that is important. I am learning about that *now* of yours. We have to live the best way we can. I know this means something different for each of us. I didn't know this method of living was applicable to all ages."

"Don, you are such a philosopher. While you are teaching me the art of detachment, I find myself getting more attached. I think suffering is all about what goes on between the ears. But, we both know, learning an art, and practicing that art is not one and the same.

"These are difficult moments in both our lives. It is difficult. I get tired, and of course, I get impatient. It is patience Dr. Gladys McGarey has been trying to teach me for years. She failed, too. Yet, there is nothing, and no one on earth who can remove me from where I am right *now*. I can try to escape a thousand times, but the fact is: I am here for the long run. That is my wish!

"As we go on that short walk of ours, I am discovering what love is. Don in all honesty, I had no idea! That stuff is powerful. I am a very lucky woman. I will do my best to bring your words and also mine to the material world. I know, in this process, I am making myself a better person. I also know the words in your stories will make others better than they were before."

"Evie, I now understand, the science of behavior opposes what most people think because of conditioning. Your conditioning did not provide you the human processes for the kind of love you express. You have a passion for life I hope you do not lose."

"Don, after many years in self-absorbed thinking I realize humans are able to make machines work with each other, yet as a species we have not yet learned to do the same with our own interactions or connectedness."

"Evie, unless there are psychological or perhaps neurological imbalances, our behavior is based on learned parental subtle training. We become acclimatized to what we experience at a young age from our parents, and we somehow simulate some aspects of what we learned.

"This is a hard process to learn or to teach because we equate high ideals to power other than our own. Eventually, I learned to govern myself only. I must for my own sanity.

"Evie, you always ask me what you can do to help. Here is a concept for you to think about. If you find the mechanism to convey this idea of governance to humanity, I will be happy."

Many Interruptions

Since time or dates no longer had a hold on our lives, keeping tabs on the workings of our existences became meaningless. There was no need to keep a schedule. Aside from a few visits to a doctor, life happened. Don was a storyteller, and he talked to me all the time. I was being infused with information, wisdom and memories. I, on the other hand, had the bad habit of interrupting him.

One day, during one of the numerous conversations, I interrupted him one time too many. Thousands of times, I needed clarity when I did not know or understand what he was talking about. Age and culture presented themselves often during stories being told of an era I knew nothing about.

He was not an impatient man, but he was a determined one. He had stories to tell me—my interruptions were distracting his thinking process.

One day, with the aid of his walker, he got up from the dining room chair, and walked toward his desk in order to get me a new yellow pad and a red pen. This time, he came back with his *stick* as well. This staff was given to him by one of his children. It was a prized possession. With it Don had gone down and up the Grand Canyon numerous times. That staff was at-hand when we got married. Before the arrival of a walker in our home, it had become an extension of his arm. He came back to the table and told me he had to think.

"You know Evie, when I stayed on the North Rim of the Grand Canyon, the staff was always with me. The people working at the Canyon, and some of the guests, noticed my white hair, my white beard and the staff. They were the first ones to call me a patriarch. I guess I was telling them stories, and exposing them to some of my wisdom. I didn't wear a robe.

"Now thinking back on the Grand Canyon scene, it is amusing that driving employees around for $5.25 an hour gave me the satisfaction my large assets did not offer."

At the canyon, Don said he had time to think. He sorted out all that he had learned. He was able to further put his life in the right perspective. He also composed poetry, most of which he lost. He wrote notes to friends and relatives. Not one was ever mailed.

The young foreign students who came during their vacation to work at the Canyon fascinated Don. Like him, they worked for minimum wages. Like him, they did not come for money. During the long conversations with them he learned every single one had read something about the spirit of the Grand Canyon. They explained, sometimes with limited English, they came to experience that *spirit*. He talked to them on long walks.

"Evie, those kids reminded me of when I was about fourteen travelling the USA. I was trying to understand the country that made my father a slave to people on a farm that used him as a laborer. He was four years old, Evie. The foreign kids came to experience a feeling, but not the history of the country."

"Don, the history of this country is sometimes a difficult one to swallow, especially if you have pacifist tendencies. I also know that we of the human race have a propensity about conquering and killing one another."

"Evie, you are right about that. Any way, thumb-up, with a letter from my mother, and one from the parish priest to say I was a good boy, and not a runaway, my first adventure began. Something akin to what the foreign kids did. I was younger that's all.

"I started that trip with my friend Carl. He was born in California. We went to the same school. Our destination was Virginia where he had a relative. It was during this trip that I learned more about being self-sufficient. I worked for meals, and often slept on a porch or in the back room of a restaurant. Carl and I had some good meals in those places. We did dishes. We cleaned floors. We did what we were asked. The exchange always was to get food, and even desserts sometimes. Evie, there was a lot of carefree joy during that trip. You know, this country was very different then. We were safe hitch hiking across the United States.

"The kids from overseas who came to work at the Grand Canyon had that same sense of adventure. They were, however, a few years older than when my adventure had began. Often they did not have the language. I realized how courageous they were. In their own way, they reminded me of myself but mostly of Joseph Campbell. They were not afraid to follow their bliss."

The winds of the canyon brought him once more the freedom to explore who he was. He read from Steinbeck to Dostoyevsky and almost anything in between. He took to the books of Joel Goldsmith who was a spiritual and mystical teacher. To his arsenal of teachings and learning from different masters, he became a student of Goldsmith's *The Infinite Way*. The time he spent at the Monastery, reading Lao Tzu and a few more, Don established and proclaimed complete harmony with self and others.

He told me it was around a clearing of pines by Point Imperial, the highest and northernmost area on the North Rim that he wrote:

Eveline Horelle Dailey

The Grand Canyon Speaks

Man walks to my edge

And silently stares,

Pauses a moment,

Then his voice fills the air . . .

Beautiful, glorious, grand and divine,

Then he humbly mutters

How insignificant his life is to mine.

Slowly he turns and walks away,

Not hearing my words as I say . . .

Man, you are the wonder of this land,

The greatest expression of the master's hand . . .

Only wind, rain and time can change a canyon's face

But man, with a thought, can change the human race . . . ...

This poem was written before my appearance in his life or that of a walker, or a wheelchair. We got married where it was written.

While I was thinking of his Grand Canyon adventure, he returned to the century-old table where we were having our quotidian cups of coffee.

"Evie when I talk to you, if you write the questions you have on this yellow pad, in red ink, I can continue my stories without losing where I was going with them. I hope you don't mind."

I could not help but smile.

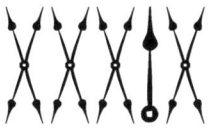

Close to Me

As we all take our lives for granted, none of us seems to know beforehand, that the energy of exhaustion does flow between people.

Lying down next to him, on his hospital bed, became one of my afternoon routines. It was a place, and a moment to restore our entire beings. Our dog Charlie, who had become his therapy dog, was always with us. It is a wonder we could breathe while on that bed.

"Don, we have a rich life. Now more than ever, I know, there is something grand about taking life a moment at a time. Knowing that we will not be alive forever gives me a sense that nothing is a matter of chance. I like the deliberate life we chose. It gives us power."

We spent most of that day talking about being deliberate. I took the time to examine his staff, this well used symbol for a patriarch. It was made from a stalk of a desert agave plant. In places where the wood had split, a skillful artisan had inserted small pieces of brilliant Birdseye Turquoise. It was after this examination that the staff had changed utility. Somehow, that day it had made its way into bed with us.

He remained immobile while I rested for twenty minutes. This communion between us could not wait for yet another breathing treatment. Twenty minutes became a religious practice. A time to rest, a time to ponder, a time to take refuge in a few synchronized breaths. Yes, the experience was extremely rich.

When I got up to begin my nursing duty, he gave me the staff, reminding me of its new purpose—it had become a *talking stick.*

"Eveline, no matter what you say or think, make attempts at practicing the art of detachment. I know you, and you must do this. Tears are a good release, but do not get stuck there. We all have purpose, and even the staff has found its resolve. By the way, I like that you tied the feathers and the pouches to the stick. You know we should not have the feathers from the hawk given to us by your friend the Native American chief."

"Well, Don, let somebody come to get them, and give them back to the bird that lost his life. Tell the driver that killed the bird and kept on going that it was a sacred bird. The person wanting the feathers back will have to deal with me. They were gifted to me. They have reason and purpose in our lives, remember that!"

Attached to the staff, I also tied our bundles—an odd word to signify a small pouch— made, with care, of kid-leather, carried herbs from the land. We gave importance to things most people took for granted or did not know about. For us the sacredness of the planet itself was contained in these objects. On American soil, I learned to respect the land where I walked.

Our common grounds were perhaps odd and unknown to friends or family. Everything around us had symbolic meaning.

As I held the staff, I learned many lessons during these precious moments.

I learned to listen, while he talked. Conversations from around the table continued every day. Solace was found where focus was layered onto the yellow pad.

Every moment was precious and meaningful.

The staff became the implement that would supply both of us the fluidity of thoughts and new discoveries were made. While we were aware that death was outside our doors, we also experienced awe.

"Evie, you are going to think I am crazy, but I do not know anyone with a bond such as ours. I am glad that somehow we were able to recognize the sanctification of words between us. When I am gone, you probably will replace me with a young stud."

"Well Don, I have to disappoint you. You will be replaced by a Doberman."

"You mean a dog? No, no, not a Doberman, Charlie would not like that.

"Eveline, do you understand that ours is a connection from our souls? I am not sure I truly understand what that is. But what I feel is a lot greater than feelings of a man for a woman."

Sometimes, all I could do was to look at him, allowing a natural flow of tears to escape. Indeed, ours was a connection of souls.

"Sweetheart, I will be gone, we know that. I will be with you in a different capacity. I will send you flowers from that space in the stars. I know you will be able to perceive the scent.

"Evie, I am so glad we are able to talk, really talk. Somehow, I know you are protected by universal light."

Friends and Family Visitation

"Evie, the art of oration is lost to a generation I can't identify with. The art of body language is lost to a screen at anyone's fingertips. The tones of voices have lost their vibrations. You know the generation after you and I will lose the precious art of dialogue. I am glad I am dying.

"I wonder if they know, as people lose their ability to communicate, they will find themselves more and more frustrated. They will get angry, they will become irrational, and, they will have ceased to feel the totality of a conversation. Words are so important when well spoken. I know when you write you attempt to clarify the abstract thoughts you have. You can't 'twixt' and do that. I watch people, Eveline, and they behave as any addict does. They must have their device on-hand. It's like a drug."

Often after his deliveries filled with wisdom, all I could do was ponder. I had to accept my impending loss was never too far. I had to look at my own mortality. I had to think of what he had just told me.

"Evie, do I bore you with what I say? I know I talk too much. With all that's going on with me, would you marry me again? Would you ask me to be your husband?"

"A thousand times I would!"

Let's Go For A Short Walk

He did not know how proud I was to be his wife. I had grown to admire every fiber of this man. My journey with him gave me the opportunity to learn not only from him, but also from the ones he had learned from. He had acquired a collection of great men and women who were teachers. Some, he met personally, and the rest through ancient written words. They were the guiding forces that carved a thoroughfare for him and also for me to walk on.

Because ours was a relation filled with conversations, we never lost the intentional focus of dialogue, nuances of moods, the movement of a pair of eyes or lips smiling, frowning or sometimes quivering in an effort to arrest some difficult emotions. Perhaps because he was a man able to express himself with words, laughter or tears I became observant of all faces including mine.

"Don, I have come to believe, in a life or a marriage when people talk, each individual traverses his or her own sea of joy and tears. Without fruitful communications people may not be able to maneuver the difficult waters they have to swim in. My heart aches for the missing elements in the lives of many."

"You know Evie, there is a road that some people take together, in our case, we took that walk with determination, candor and resolve. We have communication.

"Here we are standing around an embankment facing west. We have not talked about that clock of mine, but know this is where we can watch the sun set. In the meantime, I don't know how long I have."

I had to take a few deep breaths.

"It was not my intention to have you walk this difficult journey. Do you remember our first walk? You had gold sandals on. That too was not an easy walk for you. Somehow you did five miles. I think with your help, I can live and walk until I can't walk or live anymore. We can do it together. I am asking a great deal of you. I have told you many times, you can leave if you want."

I took another few deep breaths.

That sort of hiatus gave us a vista to examine what had become important in our lives—one of us was dying faster than the other.

I Read Some Sage.

"Evie, I hope, for a while longer, I can continue to be the center of my existence minus the infringement of my ego. I know it is alive and well. With that in mind, I hope that my seeds grow old to become wise people. Wiser than I can ever be! There is so much to wish for when we have children. Sometimes, when I meet young people I see a spark, a celestial light they don't know they have. I see this in the bright eyes of my great grandson. To me, he is a kind of silent witness of what I wish for humanity."

"Don, this is marvelous. Have you told your grandson he is part of the seeds you talk about?"

"Evie, I can't tell each of my grandchildren what I have in my heart for them. Few parents, or grandparents know how to express these things. The feelings are just there. I did write a little poem that approaches what I feel."

"Wow! Again, you elate me. I am so fortunate to be in your life and then I discover the many aspects of you. If you lived to be one hundred plus years, every day I will discover something knew."

Eveline Horelle Dailey

For my Great-Grandson

No fog no smog filled the air this day
The winter's wind blew all impurities away
It is not winter
it is spring
Treetop dancing choreographed by the wind
A rhapsody in movement is playing for me
My seed became a great-grandson
Changing cloud moving in silent disarray
The sky I see is no longer gray
It is a new life
I went to sea and walked on sand
The eye of the child I now see
Does not know it is fall in my life.

"Evie, I was feeling liberation, and those are the words that got stuck to the paper.

"There are times that I attempt to measure whatever wisdom I may have gathered. When I do this I find conflict instead of understanding. I try to see goodness, and only a glimmer of a light shines to inspire me. Those are the times that I know how important you are in my life. You have a way of shining the light and dissolving the shadows. I think I was thinking about something like that when I wrote the poem. You make the seasons of my life disappear.

"When I saw my great-grandson, I can tell you there was nothing but light around him."

"Lucky man, you can see what most people ignore. Back to the wisdom you have gathered, I dare say, it is *not* made of egotistical matter. I believe there are few men or women able to detach themselves from their manufactured self-image. That, my friend, is another one of your traits admired by many. I know I am not the only one with feelings of pride just to know you."

Eveline Horelle Dailey

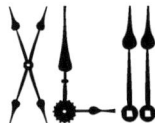

The Clock Kept Ticking

"I know I have neglected telling you more about my idea of the continuum of life as I understand it. By the way, you, my dear, never told me about that vision quest of yours. I want to know about that because, I am certain, it determined many things in your life."

"Don, I will make another deal with you. You tell me more about the clock and I will tell you about the quest. How would that work?"

"Evie, you have a way of pushing me. I don't know if that's good or bad. Get me some ice cream I'll talk until I'm done with the container."

"I do not understand how anyone can eat as much ice cream and not gain an ounce."

I got him a new box of Pralines and Cream, a spoon and a towel. He arranged his bed, his pillow, and his table just right in front of him. The towel became an enormous bib. Once all this was done, he was ready to savor the ice cream I had learned to soften in the microwave. This appliance I despised, and used only for the ice cream.

"The thing with the clock I talk about, I visualize as a continuum in my life. It is a circle that began the day I was born. The clock can't go backwards. That is one of the laws of the universe. The whole thing is a one-way trip. That, my dear, is the case for everyone, no matter how much we fool ourselves. The fact is the movement goes one-way only.

"The idea is that whatever I am looking for, I can only find ahead of where I am. I can only go forward. I can't ever find what has passed. Those are memories, they may have given me some clues about my life, but once gone, I am reminded to go forward. When a thing is gone, it is gone. The idea of living in the *now* is good to know. Where we stand is the only place from which to take steps forward."

"I am getting the clock idea. You wound it up and it goes only forward. You are onto something. Better tell me more."

"Imagine as life begins the clock is set. You can't go back. All of life works that way. I think when Giotto made his perfect circle he understood that.

"In our lives, instead of going forward all the time, we spend inordinate time thinking about what we don't have. More time is wasted thinking about what we should have. None of these things are ever possible. We give what is lacking in our lives all kinds of energy, we complain, we talk, and since everything is energy, we bring in more of that same energy around us. Like attracts like. As I have heard you say, *it is in the doing that things change.*

"Now, using the same principle, just thinking about what is wanted, the universe will deliver.

"When I wanted to have a lot of houses so I could rent them all, I visualized a steady flow of income. In my mind some houses were green and with yellow trim, and some were yellow with green trim. I had no money to buy that first house. The deal was presented in a way that I could afford it. I just kept visualizing my houses green and yellow and yellow and green. The law of attraction took over and before I knew it, I had fifty houses."

"I get that! You see, not all people can do this. They make hundreds of excuses why their lives are difficult. They do not know or admit they are fearful. You have tapped into universal flow. That's how you acquired your fortune. Yes, you are a patriarch. You just do not visualize yourself as such."

"Evie, all I know is that too often people come up with nothing but excuses. They rationalize why things can't be. Well, if that is where their energy is, nothing can grow. I think people do this because they are afraid of changes in their lives. You say fear in a broad sense is the cause of non-performance. If I can use these words, I think people are afraid of change."

"I guess you are right, Don. This is fluid energy, the stuff divine movement is made of. The stuff you know how to tap into from the cosmos."

"Evie, I do not have a name or a word for it. Here is another example for you: listen to the news. You hear about people killing people. Everybody is talking about it, they raise the energy of killings, it becomes a parlance, so of course there is going to be more killing. It is really not about crime; it is about what we give our energy to.

"Remember you read something to me, about the collective structure of the organized field of energy. It's no different than what fear is. We think of it, we become afraid; we keep on thinking about it, we have more fear. Before you know it, there is paralysis.

"Evie, when you told me a few things about the vision quest, I noticed that somehow you learned to conquer your own fears. I notice you don't nourish any fear you may have. This is something I want to investigate with you."

"Don, I never thought of it that way. I do not know where I learned not to be fearful. I know I do not fear people who are different than I am. I have a feeling the lack of fear and the ability to be daring probably came from my father. The little that I remember of him tells me he was a man without fears. He was not afraid to engage people. I think I am also like that. To know about people you must learn from them."

"Evie, at this time, there are great advantages to my station in life. I have lived a long time, and I have given my life and myself the tools to grow with and from. Some would say I am a selfish man, and that does not concern me. I live my own life, and I grow from what I learn every day."

"You live fully, yet I do not sense any attachments to things, ego and places. You keep good memories, but few sorrows. You harbor no bitterness, yet when I think of the life you had, I have a feeling *I* would be bitter."

"Evie, bitterness is a waste of time, and for sure a serious waste of energy. Now, not trying to change the subject, I just remembered to tell you something. When I was a kid, we were so poor when my parents could afford to buy each of us a piece of candy; it was a treat. Imagine that! A simple piece of candy! Today most kids spit the candy out, if they don't like color or the texture. Ice cream, which you know I love, I had maybe once a year for my birthday. So I grew up without the things I really loved. Ice cream and candy!

"I swore to myself, as an adult I would become a millionaire. There was no space for bitterness there. I knew my dream was possible. It felt like when you throw a rock into a pond and you see the ripples. I knew I had to do something like that. As I got older, that became something I knew I could do. But not with a rock.

"Even though I had studied plenty, real estate was the endeavor that brought me money. I became a broker and also had my own offices. I even became the property manager for the city. It did not take a long time and buying houses became a game.

"The thing is, I had made myself available to anyone and everyone I met. I told them what I did and how. As time went by, some people found themselves in financial jams. I bought the houses back from them. Sometimes they could no longer afford the home purchased. I would give them the amount they spent during the time they were in the house and they would deed the equity to me. These were grateful people—their credits were not affected—they got some money. I got another house.

This part of my life was also like a wheel, a circle. No matter where you look you will find a circle. I did."

"Some people would say I was careless because I could have accumulated more money. Evie, when you think of it, I had all that I needed. When I knew a family that could not afford much, I allowed them to stay in the house free of charge until they got back on their feet. Nothing new to you, I know, because I saw your own generosity.

"Evie, the thing is, I know what it is to have been poor. I would never willingly let someone go homeless. If it was not for my mother's aunt in upstate New York, we would have been homeless. I remember my mother crying. I remember the face of my father. I remember giving them all the quarters I had, they were not enough to pay the rent and buy some food. I was only a little boy, but I still remember.

"It's because I had many houses, and helped those I could, that I had forgotten about one house. I had made an arrangement with a lady who had two children. She rented the house from me and about nine months later, she lost her job. She called me to let me know she could not pay the rent. When I asked her what she was going to do, she told me she would look for another job right away. In the meantime, each of her children would have to go to a different relative and a different school. She had a car, so she could park the car at her sister's house and live there until she could again afford some rent.

"This woman was crying as she told me. Evie, I could literally hear my mother. I told her to stay where she was. It was not the first time I did that. Sometimes, people have a very hard time. This lady died not long after our conversation. Her mother, an older woman, came to be with the kids."

"Don you are such a remarkable man. You do know patriarchs have tribes. You had a long and wide one."

"Evie, I know you make fun of me. I did not tell this story to anyone. It was seventeen years later, when I was checking some tax bills, that I recognized the address of the house and realized I had not heard one word about the house, or the people. I went to pay them a visit. The grandmother, an illiterate woman, told me her daughter had passed and she was taking care of the house and the kids. They were in college.

They each had received scholarships—one was going to be a nurse and the other was going to become a lawyer. I could not help but smile. I almost cried.

"As I was getting back in my car, the younger kid came home, driving a piece of junk. She recognized me, but did not know my name. She told me more about her mother and when she had died. I had to tell her I was glad they were still living in my house. She looked at me, and she understood. 'Sir does that mean we have no rights being here?' Evie, what was I to do? Two kids in school, they must have been smart enough to get some scholarships. I told her not to worry about a thing. I made an appointment with her and her brother to meet in a week. I could only do one thing and I did. I gave them the deed to the house."

"And you never told anyone?"

"Why would I need to tell anyone? I think it was after that incident that I met that first monk. We were talking about money in general and he asked me how much money I had in my pocket. I thought the man was going to rob me. Since I always carry a $100.00 bill with me, I told him, but I had a few more dollars, about $175.00. He then asked me how much money was sufficient. My accountant had just told me I had a million dollars in assets. That was sufficient for my needs. This monk was a bright man; he asked me if I was happy.

"Evie, I had forgotten the sequence of this incident. It was not too long after that I decided to go to the abbey in New Mexico. This is where I learned it was not money that would make me happy. While I was there, one of the monks, on an afternoon when we could talk, engaged me, again with a conversation about money. I think they could tell by my clothes. Anyway, this one monk told me it was very deep inside of me that I would find happiness. The bell rang, signaling the end of talking with the monk for the day.

"For some reason, what he said triggered something else in me. I realized if I could concentrate and use my energy to buy one house after the other, I could also use the same energy to get happiness. Like the first house, I did not know where it would come from. And there I was!

"From that point on, I devoted a lot of time to finding happiness. I had to close my real estate offices. A shift had taken place inside of me. Privately, I sold some houses. I was feeling very good with what I was doing. I got to understand that my source of happiness was between my ears and in my heart. My bank account had nothing to do with any of it. I gave away two more houses. It was a time in my life that I was discovering who I was. Going to the Grand Canyon also created part of the changes in me.

"I now can honestly say I was being prepared to meet you, because really, Evie, you were a gift to me."

He looked at me with a smile. The hazel of his eyes was soft. He fixed his pillow, pushed away the hospital table holding the empty carton of ice cream.

"Evie, I am tired. I need to take a nap."

Finding the Opening

Serving his meals on the special table made for a hospital bed had become another ritual to extend the pleasures of life. Since I sewed, making appropriate napkins, and table cover was easy. Before eating I covered his chest with a warm, lightly lavender perfumed, warm towel.

Writing this, I realize often logic for what I did could be considered idiotic. But who said a couple of peculiar people could not have practical fun? Morsels of foods or drops of soup did not soil his shirt. The patriarch, unlike the biblical one, wore clean clothes every day. He was a well groomed man and at all cost this was preserved. His dignity was of utmost importance to him and also to me.

I ate with him while he pretended to eat with me. At each meal the dishes were different. He often told me I had an addictive personality. First, I could not pass on beautiful dishes, especially if they came from Germany or England. My retort to his comments was that at least I had better taste than he had. Once upon a time, he too, had his own addiction. Beer was his favorite beverage.

We managed life with music, stories, flowers and the garden. To the manner of my arrangement of our lives he often smiled, looking at me as if to say *thank you, silly woman.*

Too often he told me life was meant for living. I took him at his word.

"Evie, this week I may not be able to get you flowers. My feet are not collaborating. Will you go to Trader Joe's and get yourself some flowers? By now the orchids are back. Get some will you? I have grown to love them, too."

In three seconds I was in the car on my way to get my flowers. Additionally, I found some oatmeal from Ireland that I could not pass by. The boxes, feet away from the most glorious orchids were waiting for my hand to snatch.

Since my grandfather had told me that oats were for horses, I did not eat any. We joked about the insanity of my grandfather. Meeting him only three days in my life, I could only attest that he was rather eccentric.

Once in my kitchen, I took from the land of Don's ancestors. I prepared him a tablespoon of oatmeal, three raspberries, mostly for decoration, and I delivered him this new snack. An ounce of orange juice would perhaps entice him to eat some. He no longer drank tea or coffee, and he no longer took any vitamins or drugs for Parkinson's, kidney, heart or whatever else prescribed. He only accepted oxygen—the diseases, he said, would do what they would do.

I came to understand the role of a caretaker. I knew that it demanded the courage to accept the things that could not change. Understanding, however, was not a prerequisite for coming to terms with the developments in our lives. We proposed to live life as if all was grand.

A breathing treatment before a meal and another after had become the new routine.

From our bedroom, I looked at the brilliant rays of the Arizona sun. Don's eyes, that lately had a hard time staying open, were bright. He was neither smiling nor was he somber. He had an air of detachment.

"Evie, something has changed. The dying process has begun. I understand *The Tibetan Book of the Dead*. You know it is about living and receiving assistance to get to the other side. I am sorry, but both these duties are falling on your shoulders. I know you understand. You have a lot more strength than you give yourself credit for."

"Dailey, there are times that you really aggravate me. If you were not dying, damn it, I would kill you!"

"Would you hurt that beautiful face? Come, let's talk. Besides, you still have a story to tell me."

"Dear me! You are a pain!"

"So tell me about the vision quest and I won't bother you after."

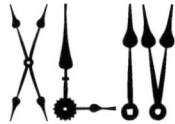

The Vision Quest

"Let me start with my seemingly overcharged life. As much as I say I do not like children, I spent a great deal of time with them teaching them to plant gardens. I was very implicated and engaged with Gardens for Humanity. I must tell you, though, the first bulb I ever planted I did so upside down. A five-year-old girl told me so. After that episode, I took some classes. I am not a master gardener. I also had the affairs of an art gallery to handle, and my own design and manufacturing companies to control as well. I was busy. Like you, I was always on a pursuit of something outside of me to bring out the inside of me.

"To the plate too full, I added one more thing. At first it was the sweat lodge. There I learned we were all the children of Grandfather Sun, and Grandmother Moon.

"You already know about the sweat lodge, remember, the *Inepe*. Two years later I was ready for the next step. For that, the preparations had been done. One evening inside the *Inepe*, four of us were told at the next full moon to bring a heavy jacket, bring good gloves, wear heavy socks and a hat, a gallon of water, and bring tissues. This appointment would not be at night but around noon. The shaman liked being mysterious, but we knew he was talking about going on a vision quest.

"At the appointed day, I was ready. Four of us got into the shaman's van, an ancient SUV that should not have been allowed on the road. We were en route to the Mogollon Rim, a place where the elevation was around 5,000 feet high—covered by a Ponderosa Pine forest. I was not at all comfortable with the idea, but I had agreed. For a short while I was under the impression that the four of us would be together. I was wrong. At one point, he stopped, got out of the driver's seat, opened the door and the first one of us was out of the van. He opened the back of the van and gave her a gallon of water. He said, 'go find your spot while the sun is out. Good luck. I will see you here exactly in seventy-two hours.' It was evident we were not going to be together."

"For a moment I thought I did not understand. He got back behind the wheel and drove another hour or so. It was my turn to get out. Same instructions; 'go find your spot, and measure the water you drink. See you in seventy-two hours.' He left me standing on the side of the road. Holding my coat, my box of tissues and my gallon of water. He got back in his SUV and drove away.

"At first I memorized where I stood. After that, I started walking a straight line. I turned to look back. All I saw were millions of pine trees and they were all around me. I could no longer see where he had dropped me off. There was a clearing in front of me, and I decided to go there. All in a straight line, I was sure of it. The sun was going down. What should have been west looked like north to me."

"Evie, I can visualize you, in a forest, with a gallon of water, a box of tissues, and a coat made for Alaska. Sorry honey, I have to laugh."

"My entire body was shaking. I did not have a watch. I did not know what time it was, but at every breath, the sun disappeared even more. The fears I never had came to the surface. The clearing was not a clearing. All around me there were tree trunks and pine needles. I could not differentiate one pine tree from another. Only the aroma was pleasant. I imagined that twelve pines made a kind of circle. I could touch each tree by taking one step. I felt this was a good clear space. It was my spot.

"I think I was tired. I could feel myself shaking a lot more. I was about to have a heart attack. I could feel my heart about to burst. I also needed to pee. I was petrified. If I lowered my pants, a bear would come running after me. I had heard a few. I speculated about the various ways I would escape. I did this for as long as I could, but I had to abide to nature. I soon understood why the shaman had suggested the box of tissue. There was just enough light to find a stick. With it I buried my tissue. I had been instructed about the way of the wild.

"I stood up and fixed my hat and my gloves, tired and still shaking. I heard a group of jaguars. I saw bears walking upright and very close to me. There were lions too. Their footprints were within feet of me. It got dark in a second. The full moon followed the sun and disappeared too. I took great care not to breathe too often. I did not want anything to hear me. I heard a rumble—elephants were on a rampage, and they too came within feet of me. I knew the sun came down to the north instead of west. I was sure of it. The moon was still nowhere to be found. I knew it followed the sun. I could tell it was not a full moon. The calendar had lied to me. There was nothing like a moon in the sky. I stayed quiet, very quiet. I could sense something right behind me. If I turned my head, it would kill me. *Very quiet, not one breath.* It was there, big with fangs and hungry for human blood. I knew it, I could feel it, I could smell it."

"Evie, did you understand the nature of your fears?"

"Fear! I am getting there. What fear? Then I saw some stars. There were no sounds. Even the beast must have been looking at them. In the forest, the constellations became up close and personal. I know the animals were around and they were surrounding me. I know they were there, not too far. They were looking at me. I heard the flight of night birds. Then I realized there was peace in the sound the wings made. I looked up to see them. I saw other stars. I was very tired.

"I woke up before the sun came out. I had no idea when I sat with my head against a tree, that within touching distance, a fawn and two little ones were still sleeping. I felt tears flowing down my cheeks. It was still dark, and I could still see some stars, perhaps fewer. One of the babies woke up and walked toward me. I was immobile, this time not because of fear. I was being careful not to breathe in a way that would frighten this fragile little one. It smelled me some, and lay back down, this time next to me. I did not move. I could feel my breath, and also the freshness of the air around me. I was surrounded by various scents of the forest. I was in a state of perplexity.

"Something I had never felt before was going on. I was comfortable. I was awed by everything I sensed. There was no fear. It took a while to realize, I was in the presence of a wild animal. I was in its forest. I was not afraid anymore. I was not shaking anymore. Without effort, I became comfortable. I was in a state of pure acceptance. I fell asleep again, a peaceful sleep.

"Do you want me to continue?"

"Yes I do, I want to hear through to the conclusion of your experience."

"When the sun came out, I woke up. I was fully awakened in a truer sense of the word. The family was gone. There was not a trace of them left to examine. Then I thought what difference would it have made if they left me some fur or some evidence that they were there? Don, I am not sure I can explain any of my feelings. I can tell you I felt lighter, fearless, but most of all, I was a comfortable in my own skin. All inner conflicts disappeared, replaced with a sense of peace. This is when I understood what fearless was. It was not opposite of combative. I sat up straight and drank some water. I decided to stretch my legs and perhaps retrace my steps from the night before.

"I walked the opposite direction from the previous afternoon. I walked a straight line. After a while, to my left, at a perfect right angle I saw the road.

"I decided I would not walk far but that I would explore the forest. This time I was carefree. The sun was out. I got thirsty, and realized I did not have my gallon of water. I panicked again, but this time, only for a short time. I could identify my center. A place I talked about often enough, but a place I could not identify. I think you know what I am saying."

"I do understand, Evie, something peaceful—you experienced something other worldly. You were able to let go of the burden of fear. Go on."

"I retraced my steps, slowly more sensing than seeing. In no time I found my gallon. I drank. I sat for a short time, and realized I could not sit through what I was feeling. I got up and walked my imaginary straight line for hours. I heard some birds and saw more deer. Far away I saw a mountain lion. He was taking in some sun and did not care about me. I got tired, made myself a bed, the way an animal would. I slept instantly. No birds of prey or any other animals came to disturb my mind. When I woke up, the sun was gone, to the west this time. I made an attempt at finding my bed from the night before, but that I could not do. It did not matter. I knew how to make a bed no matter where I was. The moon was full, and there was enough light to enjoy the shadows. Every noise I heard was not cause for fear.

"I did a lot of thinking that night, not sure about what, but I was absorbed with awe. While the first night was heavy with fears of things unknown, this night was amazement about exactly the same things.

"As the moon and the earth danced, I found myself no longer afraid. I had discovered peace. You know, Don, I wondered why I had allowed my imagination to control and trick me. I became aware that my fears were all manufactured by me. I discovered that I did not need to be afraid. If I were to perish, I would do so experiencing something I was searching for. I cannot say that I found anything of great acclaim. I only found a kind of peace I did not know existed. My peace.

"There was a transformation within me. Though I had not been groomed to fear anything, I knew I was no longer paralyzed with any fear of things unknown. Today, I say I exercise caution, but I do not experience fears.

"At one point in the afternoon, with my gallon of water almost finished, I started walking again. I cannot say I knew the directions, but I knew something. Although I had lost my bearings, I knew I was never lost. After about two hours, I guess, the road presented itself to my right. I cannot explain any of the feelings of this experience. If anything, I would say, my primal nature took over once I was able to get rid of mental fears."

"Did you pray while you were afraid and lost?"

"No I did not. I knew I had to find my own way. I knew that I was born with some kind of an inner compass, and I knew I would find it. I concentrated on that. I guess that *is* some kind of prayer. Remember, I had been prepared for this vision quest so some senses— dormant a while—allowed my inner guidance to take care of me. Of that I am certain. Call it faith if you wish. I cannot say I see the merit in calling the experience a vision quest. To me it was finding the 'I am' that I only knew from books. I think a discovery of self could be a better set of words to describe the experience I had. I also know, going on a vision quest is not something all people should do. In my case, a sort of inner illumination happened. When all fears disappeared, everything fell into place. And now here I am telling you about an experience I cannot quite explain."

"My dear Evie, you explained it to me well. I now know for certain that you will be fine when I am gone. You will miss me because we have a special soul assignment that we have gone through. I know you will be fine.

"Sweetheart, there are no accidents. Everything we do or we think of, has a lesson for us to grow from. You started out a free and adventuresome spirit and because of reasons that will show themselves, you needed to understand the nature of fear. You will never know how happy I am to know that you will be fine. Remember, you have a life to live. Live, Evie, until you can't live any more."

"Donaldo, do you want some ice cream?"

"You know how to con me. Yes, that would be nice. It's vanilla right? Remember your silly little Japanese bowl. The one you used when you had me taste your soy ice cream. That's not what I want. The next size bowl, like a soup bowl would be perfect. With some chocolate syrup."

When I came back into the room with the bowl, he asked me to sit next to him.

"Evie, may I ask you to feed me? I really don't have the strength to feed myself. I am going to eat this to please you, even if I asked for a lot more than I can consume. I don't need any more nourishment.

"Not a long time is left, Evie. I must wait as every part of me loses what was there a long time ago. Not much matters anymore. I know you will be fine and that matters to me.

"We studied about detachment. You practiced. Soon you will put the concept into action. You can do it.

"I am not dapper anymore and that bothers me. All I do is cause you a lot of work, pain and grief. I don't like that.

"I am not comfortable leaving you, but I know I must set you free so I can free myself. Evie, that's what detachment is.

"I know you can do it. Thank you for finally telling me about the Vision Quest. I will hold you in the spirit world. You will feel me. I know it, and you will know it too."

When the Time Comes

"Evie, walk me when the time comes. Don't be afraid to open the veil separating me from the other womb. Let me go through."

I understood well. In our fairly short marriage we had spent more time with each other than most people have in long marriages. I could not stop the steady flow of tears. He pushed away the hospital table that separated us and took me into his arms.

"It's okay to cry, Evie. I have no more tears, but I am fine with that. My body is doing what it needs to do."

A while later, he gently released his arms. We had no words. There was an understanding. There was a type of love I did not know I was capable of. It was my soul that was doing the loving. Part of my spirit was also dying.

"Evie, we are special, and must be grateful."

That day, he did not eat. He did not drink. The preference was to sleep. I watched while the oxygen was constantly on. There was no one to tell. His hand in mine gave me all that I needed.

I experienced the ultimate love and loss. I stayed in the room with him while he slept. Our dog did the same.

Next to our king-sized bed, in our bedroom, he slept. Perhaps to reassure me, he squeezed my hand, reaching between the bars of his hospital bed.

We both had read about detachment. Now I knew, I understood nothing at all. It was *his* journey. There was no one to tell.

"Evie, remember to tell me to go toward the *opening*, I don't want to forget. I don't want to get lost."

He would wake up just long enough for instructions.

There was a lot of silence in our home. I came to understand that his process must have begun when he told me something had changed.

When he woke up, it was another day. There was a blending of night and day. He held my hand for security I think. Perhaps it was for love. He drank a few drops of water I dispensed from an eyedropper. He slept again for a while. Soon it was time to keep him clean. My man would continue to be well groomed, always.

The transition has started, the new nurse had told me. I wanted to scream and yet I knew that my patriarch had accepted what I could not.

I sensed the line in time and the space continuum we had spoken of. It was a thin line. I understood it. I had to be the adult of responsibility. There were telephone calls to be made. We had talked about these things. We had not talked about my heart being broken. We had not talked of my spirit being shattered.

My world was permanently changing.

The head of a tribe was approaching his final moment. It was time for another kind of dialogue. I had instructions for forces I did not know.

The movement of life itself had lost its ebb and flow. For me there were struggles with unclear realities. Hundreds of times we talked about the destination. Again, in my mind, we were reading The Tibetan Book of the Dead. The time had come to escort a spirit, elsewhere. Detachment of the flesh brought attachment of souls.

A greater sense of the ending journey became real—almost comfortable. The idea of the circle was making sense. Both our clocks were going through forward motion. My hope was to escort my dying mate. Could I do it with grace?

We had come to the realization that we had become a pair of souls fastened to each other. We had no name for this transaction, and none was necessary.

"Evie, I am glad you decided to go on a short walk with me. It was a good walk."

He was having difficulty talking. I augmented the oxygen level.

"I will give you the final signal; remember, our agreement, when the clock makes its full circle."

"Go toward the opening"

On the third day, while holding his hand, the almond shaped eyes that had remained closed for days opened up wide. The beautiful hazel was clear. No expressions of pain, sorrow, or fear. There was clarity of intention. At the Hospice facility I waited.

"Go through the opening."

I felt a slight tremor, a semblance of a squeeze perhaps, the eyes closed never again to see the world.

The imaginary clock we had talked about had made its full circle.

Eveline Horelle Dailey

Epilogue

Time stood still—free of thoughts—tears flowed.

I waited for a revelation. I cannot say what I was waiting for, but I was in a state of waiting.

One late night my phone rang. The grandfather clock rang 10:45. Irritation was my first reaction. Who would dare call anyone or *me* at that hour?

Hello? I said a lot louder than my normal voice. I was making it clear to whoever was on the other line that this was not an acceptable time to call.

"Mrs. Dailey? My name is Ted, I am calling on behalf of your husband."

"Sir, whatever you are selling I am not interested and I can assure you, you do not know my husband."

I hang up! A moment later the phone rang again. Exasperated, once more I answered.

"Mrs. Dailey, please don't hang up. I know your husband passed away. I know it's late. Please Ma'am don't hang up, this is important. I am calling because before he passed, your husband helped me a great deal with my addictions. When I asked him how I could pay him for helping me, he asked me to do something for him. Please hear me out. Calling you is part of it Ma'am. Don told me that the two of you often joked that when he died you would replace him with a Doberman. He told me about the quality of your relationship. He helped me with communication in my marriage. I am calling because I must. Ma'am, your husband saved my life and my marriage."

This stranger knew what other people did not. I had to listen to him. It was true that Don and I had talked a great deal about what my life would be like after he was no longer in it. Each time jokingly, I told him I would replace him with a dog. A Doberman to be exact!

The man on the phone rambled on a while, and managed to give me a name and phone number of a trainer involved in all this. He told me that my husband had paid for a trained dog for me.

I thanked him and hung up.

I was confused—I had been married long enough to know that none of this made sense. We never exchanged presents because we had different taste. It was not like Don to arrange for such a gift—a dog. We were close but self-directed, and if I wanted another dog I would have looked for one. Actually, I had been looking for a small dog to keep Charlie company. My little dog was as depressed as I was. He needed the company of his own kind. I looked at the phone number this man had given me. I pondered about this episode. I did what I had been doing for a while. I cried myself to sleep.

Don could not have known that Charlie would be depressed. My husband did not know enough about dogs. We joked about me getting a Doberman. But it was joking. Nothing in my life was making sense. Eventually I must have fallen asleep.

I woke up holding the crushed piece of paper with the telephone number and the name of this dog person.

After two days, filled with anticipation, I made the phone call. While the phone rang I envisioned a young Doberman.

"Hello." I heard without excitement. Maybe it's a robot, I thought. Perhaps a dog trainer has no need for social skills. I gave my name, and informed I was ready to meet my Dobie.

Let's Go For A Short Walk

He repeated my name, and in a staccato mode, with not one extra word to spare, he told me he had nothing to do with Dobermans because they were no longer acceptable for military duty. Without taking a breath, he said, "I have two dogs you can look at, one is a black German Shepard and the other was a tan and black one, both females, both young, both pure bred and one needs to be yours." I guess he took a breath. "The dog will be trained to protect you as your husband paid for. Here is the address. Come to the dog compound and choose one of the two." Again I was informed that the dog and the training had been paid for.

I went on explaining that my preference was for a Doberman because I once had one. If not a Doberman I would look for a Shih Tzu because I had Charlie, who was grieving the loss of his human.

"Ma'am, this was your husband's idea. He felt you would need a companion. Your husband knew he would not be around, and you needed a protector. Ma'am, a Shih Tzu would not do the job of protecting you. When you are ready to make your choice call me. The dog will be an AKC Certified Good Citizen."

The man was done talking and hang up. I just had a conversation with a man without any manners. Perhaps, this was the way of the military. How dreadful, I thought. I smiled. I had been married to a man of words and stories. He had manners.

Still in my hand, I looked at the phone number and now an address. I did the only thing I could as a grieving widow—I cried.

What had been precious in my life was about to be replaced by a dog.

A few days later, while handling banking matters, I found a copy of a certified check to this trainer. Looking at the dollar amount I became convinced that my husband had lost his mind. I called the trainer.

We agreed on a time for me to visit the dog compound. I had never paid attention to any German Shepard. I never had any reason to. My husband had paid an exorbitant amount for a dog he would never know. I knew I was living in some sort of a parallel world but parallel to what?

I got to The Compound. What a stupid name, I thought. The man left me by my car and went inside what I would call a fort or a prison. The walls were at least twenty-four feet high; the gray of the cement blocks was capped with barbed wire all around the top. I was not allowed in—I waited. He returned with two dogs, one darker than the other. The lighter one looked at me as if to say, *what are you looking at.* I approached her. She smelled me, and sensed that I smelled like another dog. She sat and examined me further. The other dog, with a personality similar to the trainer, paid no attention to me. The dog, named Else chose me.

It took over four months to train this dog. When it was time to get her, I was told I was to continue the training.

The next day, this man came to my home to surrender the animal. Along with the dog, there was a cage, a cot, a muzzle, a tracker and a few more things. The man handed me a few pages of paper with commands I needed to learn. I looked at the typewritten pages—The words were written in German. I told him I did not speak German. He paid no attention to me and started to fill out some documents.

Charlie, my Shih-Tzu, looked at Else and approached with caution. Moments later, he guided her to my bedroom where he decided he had seen enough and went to his bed. The man told me I could call him if I needed to. Seconds later he left. The cage was closed and that poor animal did not know what to do. I opened the door she went in. I closed the door—I cried.

It was official, I had lost my husband who now had been replaced by a dog I did not like or understood. I was also to command her in a language I did not speak.

It took a while to come to my senses. I opened the cage and decided it would remain open. I called Else, she came to me, and I explained to her this was not a German house. I told her she was going to learn English. Poor thing cocked her head back and forth. I further told her that Charlie would teach her what she needed to know. I am not a dog trainer. I soon realized I had to change gear and retrain this dog to be part of my family.

In retrospect, I believe my husband had not lost his mind. Knowing my nature, he chose to give me something to occupy me—something outside of myself.

Today Else continues to be trained, she is a companion dog; she no longer gets German commands. She takes her job of protector very seriously. She has taken to protecting and looking out for Charlie as well.

Else, trained not to react to gunshot noises, is afraid of raindrops. I am certain she is prepared to attack if she judges that to be a necessity. She often walks up to me to let me know, *there is a noise outside and I am going to bark my head off.* After reading volumes, I know it is the nature of her breed: to protect.

She did not have to learn a foreign language to do that.

In the meantime, Donald, a man who had agreed not to buy me gifts, left me one, a lasting and extravagant one.

Extraordinary is the correct moniker I leave here for my husband.

Else is not a Doberman; she does not pretend to be one. She is an affectionate and protective dog that knows that her person has grown to love her.

Charlie, because of age, reminds her, that there is one alpha dog in this house.

Today while waiting for the arrival of three quarters of a century, I evaluate the many revelations and philosophies.

I am in a state of flow.

A Personal Message From The Author

Now that you've finished, I really do hope you've enjoyed it. As the author, I have one small request. Go to where ever you purchased this book and review it. If you are on Goodreads or any other reading community, do it there too. And if you got it from me directly, pick the book or ebook retailer of your choice. You can even visit my website (on the copyright page or the next page) and tell me what you think.

Good or bad, love it or hate it. Just don't ignore it. As an independent author, every review is important. Thanks.

About the Author

Eveline Horelle Dailey is quick to laughter and tears. Taking life to heart, she responds to a volcano within. She unearths the stories she must tell. She has a passion for the human spirit and its potential.

Educated overseas and in the U.S.A., Eveline's readers find French, her first language, influences and delivers texture to her prose. Design and art bring structure to her composition. She writes from the center of her emotions. When not writing, she can be found weaving, painting, or reading.

She is author of *The Drum Made from the Skin of My Systers, Lessons from the Lakeside—A Journey Toward Self Discovery* and *The Canvas—A Secret from the Holocaust*. Along with her books, Eveline's essays and articles are read internationally.

Residing in Arizona, Eveline is a member of many writers groups and several not-for-profit organizations.